Barnes & Noble Shakespeare

David Scott Kastan
Series Editor

BARNES & NOBLE SHAKESPEARE features newly edited texts of the plays prepared by the world's premiere Shakespeare scholars. Each edition provides new scholarship with an introduction, commentary, unusually full and informative notes, an account of the play as it would have been performed in Shakespeare's theaters, and an essay on how to read Shakespeare's language.

DAVID SCOTT KASTAN is the Old Dominion Foundation Professor in the Humanities at Columbia University and one of the world's leading authorities on Shakespeare.

Barnes & Noble Shakespeare
Published by Barnes & Noble
122 Fifth Avenue
New York, NY 10011
www.barnesandnoble.com/shakespeare

Image on p. 234:
By Permission of the Folger Shakespeare Library.

Library of Congress Cataloging-in-Publication Data

Shakespeare, William, 1564–1616.
  A Midsummer Night's Dream / William Shakespeare.
    p. cm. — (Barnes and Noble Shakespeare)
  Includes bibliographical references.
  ISBN-13: 978-1-4114-0038-2
  ISBN-10: 1-4114-0038-0
  1. Theseus (Greek mythology)—Drama. 2. Hippolyta (Greek mythology)
  —Drama. 3. Athens (Greece)—Drama. 4. Courtship—Drama.
  I.Title.

 PR2827.A1 2006
  822.3'3—dc22   2006018625

Printed and bound in the United States.
25

A MIDSUMMER NIGHT'S DREAM

William

SHAKESPEARE

MARIO DIGANGI

EDITOR

Barnes & Noble Shakespeare

Contents

Introduction to *A Midsummer Night's Dream*
by Mario DiGangi

A t the end of *A Midsummer Night's Dream*, the celebration of no fewer than three marriages makes good on Robin Goodfellow's promise that "Jack shall have Jill. / Nought shall go ill" (3.2.461–462). Of course, we don't really require the reassurance that the lovers' strife will resolve harmoniously from the mischievous fairy, since we know that marriages and happy endings are a staple of romantic comedy. While *A Midsummer Night's Dream* certainly fulfills our expectation that amorous intrigues will conclude with marriages, however, much of the pleasure afforded by the play resides in the conflicts and confusions that precede the achievement of marital stability. What we often most enjoy about Shakespearean comedy is whatever does "go ill" on the road to marriage, preventing Jack from having Jill, at least for a time.

In *A Midsummer Night's Dream*, the journey on the road to marital harmony gets off to an unusually bumpy start, even for a Shakespearean comedy. The play opens with a groom eagerly anticipating his wedding night, yet Duke Theseus's claim that he "wooed" (1.1.16) Hippolyta with his sword reminds us that this Amazon warrior was his enemy before she became his bride. Attempting to impose order upon his subjects, Theseus inadvertently provokes Hermia to rebel against patriarchal authority when, instead of approving her love for Lysander, he commands her to marry Demetrius, the suitor whom her father favors. Once Hermia and Lysander escape into the fairy-haunted forest, the order Theseus has tried to impose rapidly breaks down: close friends become bitter rivals, a faithful lover cruelly rejects his beloved, and a humble weaver finds himself the darling of the Fairy Queen. The restoration of social order requires the Athenians to return to the city, but the great appeal of *A Midsummer Night's Dream* lies in the forest, where lovers, artisans, and fairies collectively play out their "fond pageant" (3.2.114) of discord and desire.

In *A Midsummer Night's Dream*, desire is the force that paradoxically both fuels and derails the lovers' progress toward marriage. Desire is what the lovers believe they understand most immediately and intimately about themselves, yet they experience its overwhelming force as the sensation of being trapped in a dream or performing a role in someone else's play. Oberon's flower contains the essence of this overwhelming force. The flower's magical juice functions indiscriminately and irresistibly: it can compel any being to desire any other being. As such, the juice distills the very "soul of love," a power that respects neither human reason nor social authority (2.1.183).

Certainly, the suffering lovers in the play are fond of saying that love respects neither reason nor authority. Lysander believes that "[t]he course of true love never did run smooth," because for a romantic such as he the sign of true love is precisely the resistance it offers to authority figures and social expectations (1.1.134). Whereas Lysander and Hermia take comfort in the knowledge that true lovers have always suffered, Helena laments the suffering caused by Demetrius's rejection. Helena blames her misery on the arbitrary power of the blind boy-god Cupid, whose love-inducing arrow has apparently struck Demetrius, inflaming his passion for Hermia. In the magical and mythical world of the play, Cupid's arrow, like Oberon's flower, is not merely a symbol of love but an instrument of seduction that strikes without warning and without reason.

Readers of *A Midsummer Night's Dream* might also find themselves seduced by the appealing fantasy offered up by Oberon's flower and Cupid's arrow: the notion that the irrepressible power of love overrides all social, economic, or political considerations. The problem with this fantasy, however, is that it can prevent us from recognizing the operation of those social, economic, and political forces that direct the currents of love into acceptable channels. Even in a comedy as lyrically expressive and raucously physical as *A Midsummer Night's Dream*, love follows certain rules of social propriety. The young lovers' private feelings are subject to public standards of judgment: sometimes these standards are explicit, as when Theseus supports Egeus's patriarchal rights over Hermia; sometimes, and even more interestingly, these standards are implicit. These implicit standards—the fundamental assumptions of Shakespeare's culture regarding the social meanings of love and marriage—require a deeper look.

We might begin by considering how the play represents female virginity as both an ideal and a threat. Recounting the mythic origin of the love juice, Oberon recalls a time when Cupid's arrow failed to pierce the heart of "a fair vestal thronèd by the west"; deflected from its target, the arrow struck a white flower, turning it purple with "love's wound" (2.1.158, 167). The fair vestal is usually taken as an allusion to Queen Elizabeth I, the reigning monarch when Shakespeare wrote *A Midsummer Night's Dream*. From the beginning of her long reign, Elizabeth had resisted her counselors' urgings to get married and produce an heir to the throne. By the time of *A Midsummer Night's Dream*, she was still unmarried and past childbearing age. To justify her anomalous position as an unmarried female monarch in a patriarchal society, Queen Elizabeth shrewdly cultivated a symbolic identity as the Virgin

Queen: a modern-day manifestation of Diana, the ancient Roman goddess of chastity. Virginity carried positive associations of purity, sanctity, and inviolability—all fine qualities for a Christian monarch. Nonetheless, in Renaissance England a lifelong dedication to virginity could also be perceived as a galling resistance to the male control over female sexuality that was institutionalized through marriage.

In Oberon's tale, the chaste vestal is the exception that establishes the rule. That is, if the vestal virgin possesses the one heart out of every "hundred thousand" that is pure enough to repel sexual desire (2.1.160), then virtually all other women must be subject to love and its social consequences, namely, marriage and children. From this perspective, a woman who does not experience love for a man might be considered just as perverse as a woman (such as Hermia) who loves a man against the dictates of social and familial authority. Hence Theseus disparages virginity as a "cold" and "fruitless" state, despite the pious respect he pays to the blessed condition of nuns (1.1.73). More to the point, it is possible to understand Theseus's marriage to Hippolyta as a way of neutralizing the threat represented by the very existence of Amazons, a militaristic and self-governing nation of women who eschewed romantic ties with men. Shakespeare took the characters of Theseus and Hippolyta from Chaucer's "Knight's Tale," but he was also familiar with the overtly critical assessment of Theseus as a manipulator of women in Sir Thomas North's translation of Plutarch's *Lives of the Noble Greeks and Romans* (1579). Theseus's boast to Hippolyta—"I wooed thee with my sword / And won thy love doing thee injuries"—equates love with conquest, and thus sits uneasily with the ideal of marriage as an "everlasting bond of fellowship" between man and woman (1.1.16–17, 85). From his first lines, it is clear that Theseus desires to be married; it is harder to gauge what role romantic love plays in that desire.

To be sure, the ideal of an affectionate partnership between husband and wife was promoted in a great many English Renaissance sermons, treatises about marriage, and stage comedies. Such works acknowledge love as an important factor in achieving conjugal harmony—as long as that love does not transgress social boundaries. (Recall the trouble caused in *Othello* when a mature African general and a young Venetian noblewoman marry for love.) Oberon's flower symbolizes the radically arbitrary nature of sexual attraction, and the Athenian lovers frequently adduce the transgressive effects of desire. Yet for all that, the lovers do not violate the most fundamental distinctions of social rank. That Hermia's two alternatives, Lysander and Demetrius, are so difficult to distinguish from each other has much to do with their virtually identical social and economic status. The chaos of the forest might offer the aristocratic lovers an escape from the harshness of patriarchal law, yet it does not permit them to mix with the common artisans. Had Hermia fallen in love with Bottom, it would be difficult to imagine a harmonious conclusion for the comedy.

In *A Midsummer Night's Dream*, Shakespeare does, of course, provide an unforgettable depiction of an amorous relationship between two radically different beings: Titania, a fairy queen, and Bottom, a mortal commoner. Nonetheless, it is important to remember that Oberon drugs Titania with the love juice to punish her, not to liberate her sexually. When he names the various wild beasts that Titania might be compelled to desire, Oberon is not celebrating love's glorious ability to transcend differences between partners. After all, how might the average lion, bear, or wolf react to Titania's unsolicited amorous attentions? By bringing Titania into humiliating and potentially dangerous proximity with some "vile thing" (2.2.40), Oberon is attempting to *restore* differences, namely the superiority of the husband to the wife that was a dominant notion in Renaissance thinking about marriage. Through her refusal to relinquish the changeling boy, Titania has collapsed this marital hierarchy. Oberon restores it by substituting the "vile" Bottom for the precious changeling boy in Titania's affections. In this instance, desire becomes the means for reforming an unruly wife.

Thus for all the pleasure we might take in the erotic license at the heart of *A Midsummer Night's Dream*, the comedy's drive toward social and sexual order also offers the more mundane comfort of a return to the familiar and conventional. Ironically, at its most chaotic, Shakespeare's comic plot orchestrates the four young lovers into conventionally gendered patterns that pave the way for their impending roles as husbands and wives. We can better discern the logic of this orchestration by asking why the erotic confusion in the forest takes the particular shape it does, when another way of arranging the four lovers would have been equally plausible. Recall that Oberon intends to charm Demetrius into loving Helena, but Robin Goodfellow's application of the love juice to the wrong Athenian instead compels Lysander to desire her. Once Robin drugs Demetrius, both men pursue Helena, who believes that they have conspired to mock her, while Hermia struggles to understand Lysander's sudden change of heart.

Yet suppose that while under the influence of the love juice Lysander had awoken to see not Helena but Demetrius. At one level, such a twist would not have greatly altered the development of the comic plot as it now stands. His affections shifted to another person, Lysander would still reject Hermia, justifying Oberon's complaint that Robin has "turned" a "true love" false instead of turning a "false [love] true" (3.2.91). Lysander's sudden courtship of Demetrius, which Helena might reasonably interpret as a cruel parody of her own futile efforts to win Demetrius's love, would anger and humiliate her in the same way that Lysander's sudden courtship of her does in the play as we know it. Once enchanted by the love juice, Demetrius would form the last link in a tangled chain of error: Hermia pursuing Lysander pursuing Demetrius pursuing Helena. We know that Robin delights in things that happen "prepost'rously" (3.2.121). Etymologically, "preposterous" means back first or "ass backwards," hence inverted or in opposition to customary order. What could provide a more preposterous spectacle for Robin's (and our) entertainment than seeing Demetrius pursued by a love-struck man who used to be his rival and shunned by an exasperated woman who used to be his suitor?

Shakespeare, however, avoids such a riotously perverse scenario. Significantly, the scenario that does develop in the forest—Lysander and Demetrius both in pursuit of Helena—has the effect of sundering the friendship between the young women. The hypothetical version of the play in which Lysander dotes on Demetrius would emphasize the discomfiture of the men through the incongruous transformation of a male rival into a lover. Lysander's dotage on Helena instead generates a deep distrust between Helena and Hermia. That distrust ultimately transforms the women's long-standing friendship into a bitter rivalry, shifting their devotion from each other to their respective husbands. Shakespeare's arrangement of the lovers thus accords with the traditional goals of comedy by maneuvering the young women into their destined roles as wives.

In a passionate speech that can be regarded as the emotional core of the play, Helena accuses Hermia of betraying their "ancient love" by conspiring with men to harm her (3.2.215). It is precisely at this moment that Shakespeare abandons the highly patterned rhymed couplets in which the lovers have been communicating since Lysander and Hermia first entered the forest in Act Two, scene two. Speaking instead in the more naturalistic, genuine-sounding idiom of blank verse, Helena poignantly recalls her friendship with Hermia as an emotional, spiritual, and even erotic melding of "two seeming bodies but one heart,": "So we grew together, / Like to a double cherry—seeming parted / But yet an union in partition— / Two lovely berries molded on one stem" (3.2.212, 208–211). Singing and sewing together, Hermia and Helena had achieved the skill of "two artificial gods," their feminine creative energies rivaling the masculine creative energies Theseus attributes to Egeus, the "god" who "composed [Hermia's] beauties" (3.2.203; 1.1.47–48). Hermia and Helena had once confounded physical difference through their profound intimacy: "As if our hands, our sides, voices, and minds / Had been incorporate" (3.2.207–208). Now each woman spitefully insists on the physical and moral differences that distinguish her from her rival.

Despite all the discord that accompanies the shuffling of the young lovers into their proverbial slots as Jacks and Jills, future husbands and wives, the play sustains our confidence that Oberon's directorial manipulations will yield the "gentle concord" we expect from a comic ending (4.1.142). Indeed, part of the play's brilliance lies in the success with which its shimmering surface of magic transformations and shifting erotic geometries distracts us from paying too much conscious attention to the social imperatives of comic form that determine its shape. The farcical confusion of the central forest scenes is genuinely amusing, the insults delightfully inventive and acerbic, and nobody, after all, comes to serious harm. Retrospectively, the lovers' trials in the forest can be perceived as a ritual passage through what Oberon calls "night-rule" (3.2.5): a period of turmoil during which the deep cravings, doubts, and anxieties that accompany a difficult transition into a new stage of life might be openly, if temporarily, expressed. In a more modern idiom, we might adopt the Freudian explanation of the function of dreams in dramatizing unconscious thoughts, thereby expressing in a disguised and less threatening form those disturbing truths that the waking mind vigilantly represses for our own protection.

Thanks to Oberon's benevolent decree that the Athenians should remember "this night's accidents" as no more than "the fierce vexation of a dream" (4.1.67–68), the four lovers need not confront the anxieties, betrayals, and jealousies that have steered them into two sets of marriageable couples. Lysander remembers only that he came with Hermia into the forest in order to elope. Still under the influence of the love juice, Demetrius explains the restoration of his affection for Helena as a natural process. He compares his love for Hermia to a childish toy he has outgrown or a sickness from which he has recovered "as in health, come to [his] natural taste" (4.1.173). In a seemingly arbitrary reversal of his earlier severity, Theseus ratifies this unexpected concord by overruling Egeus's patriarchal rights over Hermia. Nor does the departure of the authority figures enable the lovers to reach a more frank understanding of events. Demetrius marvels, "These things seem small and undistinguishable, / Like far-off mountains turnèd into clouds"; Hermia concurs: "Methinks I see these things with parted eye, / When everything seems double" (4.1.186–189). In this case, to have weakened or blurred vision is a blessing. To see clearly, as Titania does when Oberon reveals the ass-headed mortal lying by her side, is to be denied the comfort of attributing an unsettling experience to the imaginary delusions of a dream. Unlike Titania, the lovers remain in suspended admiration, marveling at the neat resolution of their conflicts and spared from having to recognize at what price such a resolution has come about.

And what does Bottom recall of his night in the forest with the Fairy Queen? Bottom's recollection of his "dream" fills him with pleasure and wonder. However, Bottom also mystifies his experience, casting what has transpired during the night as beyond his comprehension. Jumbling a biblical passage in which Saint Paul affirms that God's mysteries cannot be known through sensory perception, Bottom falteringly associates his strange physical transformation into an ass with the profound spiritual transformations enacted by Christian grace. "Bottom's Dream" thus gestures toward the unfathomable profundity of a vision with "no bottom" (4.1.213, 214).

Nonetheless, Bottom's transformation into an ass was no ethereal vision or state of spiritual transcendence. Rather, that transformation involved the intensely embodied sensory experiences both of the character and of the playgoers, who are fully aware of the blatantly theatrical effects (a prop head, braying noises) necessary to represent such a magical transformation on stage. Bottom claims that a man would have to be an ass, metaphorically speaking, to believe in the literal truth of his transformation into an ass. We have willingly "believed" that truth in the superior knowledge that not fairy magic but our own theatrical imaginations have turned an actor with a costume into an ass-headed man. Whatever it has meant to him, however uplifting or humiliating its effects, Bottom's dream of an encounter with the fairies has, in some sense, liberated and empowered *us*.

Apart from a vision that he cannot or will not articulate, what Bottom is left with after his night in the forest is an opportunity. That opportunity involves another transformation, not as the passive subject of a magic spell but as the active agent of his own theatrical imagination. What, exactly, does the opportunity to perform "Pyramus and Thisbe" mean to the artisans? Like the lovers in their audience, the artisans are motivated both by pleasure and by material concerns. Significantly, whereas Shakespeare's gentle lovers do not demonstrate any overt awareness of the social and economic realities that shape their amorous desires, the artisans regard their performance of a play about gentle lovers as an opportunity for social and economic advancement. (The rejected performers who evidently intended to satirize the court's lack of support for the arts go about the same goal in an overtly confrontational mode; Theseus will have none of this.) Snug anticipates an ample reward for their efforts. Flute asserts that the Duke will give Bottom a lifetime pension of sixpence a day for playing Pyramus, although nowhere does the Duke confirm such an arrangement. Bottom himself seems motivated less by material rewards than by the sheer pleasure and power of performing. Theatrical performance allows Bottom to go beyond his own prosaic identity ("let me play Thisbe too!" [1.2.45]); to manipulate others' emotions ("let the audience look to their eyes. I will move storms" [1.2.21–22]); and to enjoy public acclaim ("I do not doubt but to hear them say, 'It is a sweet comedy'" [4.2.36–37]). In the event, it is difficult to determine how much satisfaction the artisans take from their performance, since Shakespeare allows for many possible ways of imagining the actors' responses to their audience's mocking commentary. Are they confused? injured? oblivious? undeterred?

As someone who holds the imagination responsible for mental delusions and socially disruptive fantasies, Duke Theseus is hardly the ideal spectator for a performance that so greatly depends on its audience's imagination to amend its faults. Granted, Theseus's dismissal of the lovers' story about their night in the forest as "More strange than true" provokes a mild objection from Hippolyta, who suggests that even the strangest stories can convey "something of great constancy" (5.1.2, 26). Yet even Hippolyta's more generous appraisal of the imagination does not mean that this courtly audience is prepared to receive "Pyramus and Thisbe" as anything more than an entertainment to pass the time or an expression of the commoners' humble tribute.

To be sure, "Pyramus and Thisbe" is dreadful theater. Even so, it might have more substantial insights to offer about the workings of Athenian (and Elizabethan) society than its audience realizes. Were he able to acknowledge that truth can appear in strange guises, Theseus might acquire some understanding of the social tensions in his dukedom from Quince's mispunctuated prologue, which asserts, arguably more unconsciously than incompetently, that the actors have come not to please but to offend their superiors. (Shakespeare has already broached this social tension through scenes in which the actors worry that they will be hanged if their representation of the lion or of Pyramus's suicide frightens the ladies.) Were they not so intent on impressing the Duke with their witty barbs against the actors, Lysander and Demetrius might see in the death of Pyramus and Thisbe an image of the tragic fate they themselves were fortunate enough to escape. Thisbe's faithful love might have elicited a sympathetic reaction from Helena and Hermia, did not the social conventions of Duke Theseus's court require the public silence of young women.

Perhaps such serious considerations seem incompatible with the levity Shakespeare brings to the resolution of this comedy. Without doubt, "Pyramus and Thisbe" provides an uproariously funny conclusion to what generations of readers and theatergoers have found to be a delightfully lyrical, ingenious, and entertaining play. Moreover, the unexpected return of the fairies in the last scene of the play suggests that for the comedy to end on a truly harmonious note, the audience must collectively reaffirm its "belief" in what it knows to be a purely theatrical fantasy.

But in reeling us back into that seductive world of collective imagination—the essence of theater itself—the fairies might be pulling off another one of their tricks. For if we respond uncritically and naïvely to the play's harmonious vision of benevolent fairies, joyous lovers, indulgent rulers, and endearing artisans, we risk losing sight of the social and gender norms that structure the play's comic form. In short, if we respond to the play like Bottom himself might, with genial and mystified pleasure, we might forget why the play cannot end with Bottom the weaver married to Hermia the gentlewoman. We cannot truly appreciate the pleasures of a sweet dream until we have awoken from it.

Shakespeare and His England
by David Scott Kastan

S hakespeare is a household name, one of those few that don't need a first name to be instantly recognized. His first name was, of course, William, and he (and it, in its Latin form, *Gulielmus*) first came to public notice on April 26, 1564, when his baptism was recorded in the parish church of Stratford-upon-Avon, a small market town about ninety miles northwest of London. It isn't known exactly when he was born, although traditionally his birthday is taken to be April 23rd. It is a convenient date (perhaps too convenient) because that was the date of his death in 1616, as well as the date of St. George's Day, the annual feast day of England's patron saint. It is possible Shakespeare was born on the 23rd; no doubt he was born within a day or two of that date. In a time of high rates of infant mortality, parents would not wait long after a baby's birth for the baptism. Twenty percent of all children would die before their first birthday.

Life in 1564, not just for infants, was conspicuously vulnerable. If one lived to age fifteen, one was likely to live into one's fifties, but probably no more than 60 percent of those born lived past their mid-teens. Whole towns could be ravaged by epidemic disease. In 1563, the year before Shakespeare was born, an outbreak of plague claimed over one third of the population of London. Fire, too, was a constant threat; the thatched roofs of many houses were highly flammable, as well as offering handy nesting places for insects and rats. Serious crop failures in several years of the decade of the 1560s created food shortages, severe enough in many cases to lead to the starvation of the elderly and the infirm, and lowering the resistances of many others so that between 1536 and 1560 influenza claimed over 200,000 lives.

Shakespeare's own family in many ways reflected these unsettling realities. He was one of eight children, two of whom did not survive their first year, one of whom died at age eight; one lived to twenty-seven, while the four surviving siblings died at ages ranging from Edmund's thirty-nine to William's own fifty-two years. William married at an unusually early age. He was only eighteen, though his wife was twenty-six, almost exactly the norm of the day for women, though men normally married also in their mid- to late twenties. Shakespeare's wife Anne was already pregnant at the time that the marriage was formally confirmed, and a daughter, Susanna, was born six months later, in May 1583. Two years later, she gave birth to twins, Hamnet and Judith. Hamnet would die in his eleventh year.

If life was always at risk from what Shakespeare would later call "the thousand natural shocks / That flesh is heir to" (*Hamlet*, 3.1.61–62), the incessant threats to peace were no less unnerving, if usually less immediately life threatening. There were almost daily rumors of foreign invasion and civil war as the Protestant Queen Elizabeth assumed the crown in 1558 upon the death of her Catholic half sister, Mary. Mary's reign had been marked by the public burnings of Protestant "heretics," by the seeming subordination of England to Spain, and by a commitment to a ruinous war with France, that, among its other effects, fueled inflation and encouraged a debasing of the currency. If, for many, Elizabeth represented the hopes for a peaceful and prosperous Protestant future, it seemed unlikely in the early days of her rule that the young monarch could hold her England together against the twin menace of the powerful Catholic monarchies of Europe and the significant part of her own population who were reluctant to give up their old faith. No wonder the Queen's principal secretary saw England in the early years of Elizabeth's rule as a land surrounded by "perils many, great and imminent."

In Stratford-upon-Avon, it might often have been easy to forget what threatened from without. The simple rural life, shared by about 90 percent of the English populace, had its reassuring natural rhythms and delights. Life was structured by the daily rising and setting of the sun, and by the change of seasons. Crops were planted and harvested; livestock was bred, its young delivered; sheep were sheared, some livestock slaughtered. Market days and fairs saw the produce and crafts of the town arrayed as people came to sell and shop—and be entertained by musicians, dancers, and troupes of actors. But even in Stratford, the lurking tensions and dangers could be daily sensed. A few months before Shakespeare was born, there had been a shocking "defacing" of images in the church, as workmen, not content merely to whitewash over the religious paintings decorating the interior as they were ordered, gouged large holes in those felt to be too "Catholic"; a few months after Shakespeare's birth, the register of the same church records another deadly outbreak of plague. The sleepy market town on the northern bank of the gently flowing river Avon was not immune from the menace of the world that surrounded it.

This was the world into which Shakespeare was born. England at his birth was still poor and backward, a fringe nation on the periphery of Europe. English itself was a minor language, hardly spoken outside of the country's borders. Religious tension was inescapable, as the old Catholic faith was trying determinedly to hold on, even as Protestantism was once again anxiously trying to establish itself as the national religion. The country knew itself vulnerable to serious threats both from without and from within. In 1562, the young Queen, upon whom so many people's hopes rested, almost fell victim to smallpox, and in 1569 a revolt of the Northern earls tried to remove her from power and restore Catholicism as the national religion. The following year, Pope Pius V pronounced the excommunication of "Elizabeth, the pretended queen of England" and forbade Catholic subjects obedience to the monarch on pain of their own excommunication. "Now we are in an evil way and going to the devil," wrote one clergyman, "and have all nations in our necks."

It was a world of dearth, danger, and domestic unrest. Yet it would soon dramatically change, and Shakespeare's literary contribution would, for future generations, come to be seen as a significant measure of England's remarkable transformation. In the course of Shakespeare's life, England, hitherto an unsophisticated and under-developed backwater acting as a bit player in the momentous political dramas taking place on the European continent, became a confident, prosperous, global presence. But this new world was only accidentally, as it is often known today, "The Age of Shakespeare." To the degree that historical change rests in the hands of any individual, credit must be given to the Queen. This new world arguably was "The Age of Elizabeth," even if it was not the Elizabethan Golden Age, as it has often been portrayed.

The young Queen quickly imposed her personality upon the nation. She had talented councilors around her, all with strong ties to her of friendship or blood, but the direction of government was her own. She was strong willed and cautious, certain of her right to rule and convinced that stability was her greatest responsibility. The result may very well have been, as historians have often charged, that important issues facing England were never dealt with head-on and left to her successors to settle, but it meant also that she was able to keep her England unified and for the most part at peace.

Religion posed her greatest challenge, though it is important to keep in mind that in this period, as an official at Elizabeth's court said, "Religion and the commonwealth cannot be parted asunder." Faith then was not the largely voluntary commitment it is today, nor was there any idea of some separation of church and state. Religion was literally a matter of life and death, of salvation and damnation, and the Church was the Church of England. Obedience to it was not only a matter of conscience but also of law. It was the single issue on which the nation was most likely to be torn apart.

Elizabeth's great achievement was that she was successful in ensuring that the Church of England became formally a Protestant Church, but she did so without either driving most of her Catholic subjects to sedition or alienating the more radical Protestant community. The so-called "Elizabethan Settlement" forged a broad Christian community of what has been called prayer-book Protestantism, even as many of its practitioners retained, as a clergyman said, "still a smack and savor of popish principles." If there were forces on both sides who were uncomfortable with the Settlement—committed Protestants, who wanted to do away with all vestiges of the old faith, and convinced Catholics, who continued to swear their allegiance to Rome—the majority of the country, as she hoped, found ways to live comfortably both within the law and within their faith. In 1571, she wrote to the Duke of Anjou that the forms of worship she recommended would "not properly compel any man to alter his opinion in the great matters now in controversy in the Church." The official toleration of religious ambiguity, as well as the familiar experience of an official change of state religion accompanying the crowning of a new monarch, produced a world where the familiar labels of Protestant and Catholic failed to define the forms of faith that most English people practiced. But for Elizabeth, most matters of faith could be left to individuals, as long as the Church itself, and Elizabeth's position at its head, would remain unchallenged.

In international affairs, she was no less successful with her pragmatism and willingness to pursue limited goals. A complex mix of prudential concerns about religion, the economy, and national security drove her foreign policy. She did not have imperial ambitions; in the main, she wanted only to be sure there would be no invasion of England and to encourage English trade. In the event, both goals brought England into conflict with Spain, determining the increasingly anti-Catholic tendencies of English foreign policy and, almost accidentally, England's emergence as a world power. When Elizabeth came to the throne, England was in many ways a mere satellite nation to the Netherlands, which was part of the Hapsburg Empire that the Catholic Philip II (who had briefly and unhappily been married to her predecessor and half sister, Queen Mary) ruled from Spain; by the end of her reign England was Spain's most bitter rival.

The transformation of Spain from ally to enemy came in a series of small steps (or missteps), no one of which was intended to produce what in the end came to pass. A series of posturings and provocations on both sides led to the rupture. In 1568, things moved to their breaking point, as the English confiscated a large shipment of gold that the Spanish were sending to their troops in the Netherlands. The following year saw the revolt of the Catholic earls in Northern England, followed by the papal excommunication of the Queen in 1570, both of which were by many in England assumed to be at the initiative, or at very least with the tacit support, of Philip. In fact he was not involved, but England under Elizabeth would never again think of Spain as a loyal friend or reliable ally. Indeed, Spain quickly became its mortal enemy. Protestant Dutch rebels had been opposing the Spanish domination of the Netherlands since the early 1560s, but, other than periodic financial support, Elizabeth had done little to encourage them. But in 1585, she sent troops under the command of the Earl of Leicester to support the Dutch rebels against the Spanish. Philip decided then to launch a full-scale attack on England, with the aim of deposing Elizabeth and restoring the Catholic faith. An English assault on Cadiz in 1587 destroyed a number of Spanish ships, postponing Philip's plans, but in the summer of 1588 the mightiest navy in the world, Philip's grand armada, with 132 ships and 30,493 sailors and troops, sailed for England.

By all rights, it should have been a successful invasion, but a combination of questionable Spanish tactics and a fortunate shift of wind resulted in one of England's greatest victories. The English had twice failed to intercept the armada off the coast of Portugal, and the Spanish fleet made its way to England, almost catching the English ships resupplying in Plymouth. The English navy was on its heels, when conveniently the Spanish admiral decided to anchor in the English Channel off the French port of Calais to wait for additional troops coming from the Netherlands. The English attacked with fireships, sinking four Spanish galleons, and strong winds from the south prevented an effective counterattack from the Spanish. The Spanish fleet was pushed into the North Sea, where it regrouped and decided its safest course was to attempt the difficult voyage home around Scotland and Ireland, losing almost half its ships on the way. For many in England the improbable victory was a miracle, evidence of God's favor for Elizabeth and the Protestant nation. Though war with Spain would not end for another fifteen years, the victory over the armada turned England almost overnight into a major world power, buoyed by confidence that they were chosen by God and, more tangibly, by a navy that could compete for control of the seas.

From a backward and insignificant Hapsburg satellite, Elizabeth's England had become, almost by accident, the leader of Protestant Europe. But if the victory over the armada signaled England's new place in the world, it hardly marked the end of England's travails. The economy, which initially was fueled by the military buildup, in the early 1590s fell victim to inflation, heavy taxation to support the war with Spain, the inevitable wartime disruptions of trade, as well as crop failures and a general economic downturn in Europe. Ireland, over which England had been attempting to impose its rule since 1168, continued to be a source of trouble and great expense (in some years costing the crown nearly one fifth of its total revenues). Even when the most organized of the rebellions, begun in 1594 and led by Hugh O'Neill, Earl of Tyrone, formally ended in 1603, peace and stability had not been achieved.

But perhaps the greatest instability came from the uncertainty over the succession, an uncertainty that marked Elizabeth's reign from its beginning. Her near death from smallpox in 1562 reminded the nation that an unmarried queen could not insure the succession, and Elizabeth was under constant pressure to marry and produce an heir. She was always aware of and deeply resented the pressure, announcing as early as 1559: "this shall be for me sufficient that a marble stone shall declare that a queen, having reigned such a time, lived and died a virgin." If, however, it was for her "sufficient," it was not so for her advisors and for much of the nation, who hoped she would wed. Arguably Elizabeth was the wiser, knowing that her unmarried hand was a political advantage, allowing her to diffuse threats or create alliances with the seeming possibility of a match. But as with so much in her reign, the strategy bought temporary stability at the price of longer-term solutions.

By the mid 1590s, it was clear that she would die unmarried and without an heir, and various candidates were positioning themselves to succeed her. Enough anxiety was produced that all published debate about the succession was forbidden by law. There was no direct descendant of the English crown to claim rule, and all the claimants had to reach well back into their family history to find some legitimacy. The best genealogical claim belonged to King James VI of Scotland. His mother, Mary, Queen of Scots, was the granddaughter of James IV of Scotland and Margaret Tudor, sister to Elizabeth's father, Henry VIII. Though James had right on his side, he was, it must be remembered, a foreigner. Scotland shared the island with England but was a separate nation. Great Britain, the union of England and Scotland, would not exist formally until 1707, but with Elizabeth's death early in the morning of March 24, 1603, surprisingly uneventfully the thirty-seven-year-old James succeeded to the English throne. Two nations, one king: King James VI of Scotland, King James I of England.

Most of his English subjects initially greeted the announcement of their new monarch with delight, relieved that the crown had successfully been transferred without any major disruption and reassured that the new King was married with two living sons. However, quickly many became disenchanted with a foreign King who spoke English with a heavy accent, and dismayed even further by the influx of Scots in positions of power. Nonetheless, the new King's greatest political liability may well have been less a matter of nationality than of temperament: he had none of Elizabeth's skill and ease in publicly wooing her subjects. The Venetian ambassador wrote back to the doge that the new King was unwilling to "caress the people, nor make them that good cheer the late Queen did, whereby she won their loves."

He was aloof and largely uninterested in the daily activities of governing, but he was interested in political theory and strongly committed to the cause of peace. Although a steadfast Protestant, he lacked the reflexive anti-Catholicism of many of his subjects. In England, he achieved a broadly consensual community of Protestants. The so-called King James Bible, the famous translation published first in 1611, was the result of a widespread desire to have an English Bible that spoke to all the nation, transcending the religious divisions that had placed three different translations in the hands of his subjects. Internationally, he styled himself *Rex Pacificus* (the peace-loving king). In 1604, the Treaty of London brought Elizabeth's war with Spain formally to an end, and over the next decade he worked to bring about political marriages that might cement stable alliances. In 1613, he married his daughter to the leader of the German Protestants, while the following year he began discussions with Catholic Spain to marry his son to the Infanta Maria. After some ten years of negotiations, James's hopes for what was known as the Spanish match were finally abandoned, much to the delight of the nation, whose long-felt fear and hatred for Spain outweighed the subtle political logic behind the plan.

But if James sought stability and peace, and for the most part succeeded in his aims (at least until 1618, when the bitter religio-political conflicts on the European continent swirled well out of the

King's control), he never really achieved concord and cohesion. He ruled over two kingdoms that did not know, like, or even want to understand one another, and his rule did little to bring them closer together. His England remained separate from his Scotland, even as he ruled over both. And even his England remained self divided, as in truth it always was under Elizabeth, ever more a nation of prosperity and influence but still one forged out of deep-rooted divisions of means, faiths, and allegiances that made the very nature of English identity a matter of confusion and concern. Arguably this is the very condition of great drama—sufficient peace and prosperity to support a theater industry and sufficient provocation in the troubling uncertainties about what the nation was and what fundamentally mattered to its people to inspire plays that would offer tentative solutions or at the very least make the troubling questions articulate and moving.

Nine years before James would die in 1625, Shakespeare died, having returned from London to the small market town in which he was born. If London, now a thriving modern metropolis of well over 200,000 people, had, like the nation itself, been transformed in the course of his life, the Warwickshire market town still was much the same. The house in which Shakespeare was born still stood, as did the church in which he was baptized and the school in which he learned to read and write. The river Avon still ran slowly along the town's southern limits. What had changed was that Shakespeare was now its most famous citizen, and, although it would take more than another 100 years to fully achieve this, he would in time become England's, for having turned the great ethical, social, and political issues of his own age into plays that would live forever.

William Shakespeare: A Chronology

1558   **November 17: Queen Elizabeth crowned**

1564   April 26: Shakespeare baptized, third child born to John Shakespeare and Mary Arden

1564   **May 27: Death of Jean Calvin in Geneva**

1565   John Shakespeare elected alderman in Stratford-upon-Avon

1568   **Publication of the Bishops' Bible**

1568   September 4: John Shakespeare elected Bailiff of Stratford-upon-Avon

1569   **Northern Rebellion**

1570   **Queen Elizabeth excommunicated by the Pope**

1572   **August 24: St. Bartholomew's Day Massacre in Paris**

1576   **The Theatre is built in Shoreditch**

1577–1580   **Sir Francis Drake sails around the world**

1582   November 27: Shakespeare and Anne Hathaway married (Shakespeare is 18)

1583   Queen's Men formed

1583   May 26: Shakespeare's daughter, Susanna, baptized

1584   **Failure of the Virginia Colony**

1585   February 2: Twins, Hamnet and Judith, baptized (Shakespeare is 20)

1586   **Babington Plot to dethrone Elizabeth and replace her with Mary, Queen of Scots**

1587   **February 8: Execution of Mary, Queen of Scots**

1587   **Rose Theatre built**

1588   **August: Defeat of the Spanish armada** (Shakespeare is 24)

1588   **September 4: Death of Robert Dudley, Earl of Leicester**

1590   **First three books of Spenser's *Faerie Queene* published; Marlowe's *Tamburlaine* published**

1592   March 3: *Henry VI, Part One* performed at the Rose Theatre (Shakespeare is 27)

1593   **February–November: Theaters closed because of plague**

1593   Publication of *Venus and Adonis*

1594   Publication of *Titus Andronicus*, first play by Shakespeare to appear in print (though anonymously)

1594   Lord Chamberlain's Men formed

1595   March 15: Payment made to Shakespeare, Will Kemp, and Richard Burbage for performances at court in December, 1594

1595   **Swan Theatre built**

1596   **Books 4–6 of *The Faerie Queene* published**

1596   August 11: Burial of Shakespeare's son, Hamnet (Shakespeare is 32)

1596–1599   Shakespeare living in St. Helen's, Bishopsgate, London

1596   October 20: Grant of Arms to John Shakespeare

1597   May 4: Shakespeare purchases New Place, one of the two largest houses in Stratford (Shakespeare is 33)

1598   Publication of *Love's Labor's Lost*, first extant play with Shakespeare's name on the title page

1598   Publication of Francis Meres's *Palladis Tamia*, citing Shakespeare as "the best for Comedy and Tragedy" among English writers

1599   Opening of the Globe Theatre

1601   February 7: Lord Chamberlain's Men paid 40 shillings to play *Richard II* by supporters of the Earl of Essex, the day before his abortive rebellion

1601   February 17: Execution of Robert Devereaux, Earl of Essex

1601   September 8: Burial of John Shakespeare

1602   May 1: Shakespeare buys 107 acres of farmland in Stratford

1603   March 24: Queen Elizabeth dies; James VI of Scotland succeeds as James I of England (Shakespeare is 39)

1603   May 19: Lord Chamberlain's Men reformed as the King's Men

1604   Shakespeare living with the Mountjoys, a French Huguenot family, in Cripplegate, London

1604   First edition of Marlowe's *Dr. Faustus* published (written c. 1589)

1604   March 15: Shakespeare named among "players" given scarlet cloth to wear at royal procession of King James

1604   Publication of authorized version of *Hamlet* (Shakespeare is 40)

1605   Gunpowder Plot

1605   June 5: Marriage of Susanna Shakespeare to John Hall

1608   Publication of *King Lear* (Shakespeare is 44)

1608–1609   Acquisition of indoor Blackfriars Theatre by King's Men

1609	*Sonnets* published
1611	**King James Bible published** (Shakespeare is 47)
1612	**November 6: Death of Henry, eldest son of King James**
1613	**February 14: Marriage of King James's daughter Elizabeth to Frederick, the Elector Palatine**
1613	March 10: Shakespeare, with some associates, buys gatehouse in Blackfriars, London
1613	**June 29: Fire burns the Globe Theatre**
1614	**Rebuilt Globe reopens**
1616	February 10: Marriage of Judith Shakespeare to Thomas Quiney
1616	March 25: Shakespeare's will signed
1616	April 23: Shakespeare dies (age 52)
1616	**April 23: Cervantes dies in Madrid**
1616	April 25: Shakespeare buried in Holy Trinity Church in Stratford-upon-Avon
1623	August 6: Death of Anne Shakespeare
1623	**October: Prince Charles, King James's son, returns from Madrid, having failed to arrange his marriage to Maria Anna, Infanta of Spain**
1623	First Folio published with 36 plays (18 never previously published)

Words, Words, Words: Understanding Shakespeare's Language
by David Scott Kastan

I t is silly to pretend that it is easy to read Shakespeare. Reading Shakespeare isn't like picking up a copy of *USA Today* or *The New Yorker*, or even F. Scott Fitzgerald's *Great Gatsby* or Toni Morrison's *Beloved*. It is hard work, because the language is often unfamiliar to us and because it is more concentrated than we are used to. In the theater it is usually a bit easier. Actors can clarify meanings with gestures and actions, allowing us to get the general sense of what is going on, if not every nuance of the language that is spoken. "Action is eloquence," as Volumnia puts it in *Coriolanus*, "and the eyes of th' ignorant / More learnèd than the ears" (3.276–277). Yet the real greatness of Shakespeare rests not on "the general sense" of his plays but on the specificity and suggestiveness of the words in which they are written. It is through language that the plays' full dramatic power is realized, and it is that rich and robust language, often pushed by Shakespeare to the very limits of intelligibility, that we must learn to understand. But we can come to understand it (and enjoy it), and this essay is designed to help.

Even experienced readers and playgoers need help. They often find that his words are difficult to comprehend. Shakespeare sometimes uses words no longer current in English or with meanings that have changed. He regularly multiplies words where seemingly one might do as well or even better. He characteristically writes sentences that are syntactically complicated and imaginatively dense. And it isn't just we, removed by some 400 years from his world, who find him difficult to read; in his own time, his friends and fellow actors knew Shakespeare was hard. As two of them, John Hemings and Henry Condell, put it in their prefatory remarks to Shakespeare's First Folio in 1623, "read him, therefore, and again and again; and if then you do not like him, surely you are in some manifest danger not to understand him."

From the very beginning, then, it was obvious that the plays both deserve and demand not only careful reading but continued re-reading—and that not to read Shakespeare with all the attention a reader can bring to bear on the language is almost to guarantee that a reader will not "understand him" and remain among those who "do not like him." But Shakespeare's colleagues were nonetheless confident that the plays exerted an attraction strong enough to ensure and reward the concentration of their readers, confident, as they say, that in them "you will find enough, both to draw and hold you." The plays do exert a kind of magnetic pull, and have successfully drawn in and held readers for over 400 years.

Once we are drawn in, we confront a world of words that does not always immediately yield its delights; but it will—once we learn to see what is demanded of us. Words in Shakespeare do a lot, arguably more than anyone else has ever asked them to do. In part, it is because he needed his words to do many things at once. His stage had no sets and few props, so his words are all we have to enable us to imagine what his characters see. And they also allow us to see what the characters don't see, especially about themselves. The words are vivid and immediate, as well as complexly layered and psychologically suggestive. The difficulties they pose are not the "thee's" and "thou's" or "prithee's" and "doth's" that obviously mark the chronological distance between Shakespeare and us. When

Gertrude says to Hamlet, "thou hast thy father much offended" (3.4.8), we have no difficulty understanding her chiding, though we might miss that her use of the "thou" form of the pronoun expresses an intimacy that Hamlet pointedly refuses with his reply: "Mother, *you* have my father much offended" (3.4.9; italics mine).

Most deceptive are words that look the same as words we know but now mean something different. Words often change meanings over time. When Horatio and the soldiers try to stop Hamlet as he chases after the Ghost, Hamlet pushes past them and says, "I'll make a ghost of him that lets me" (1.4.85). It seems an odd thing to say. Why should he threaten someone who "lets" him do what he wants to do? But here "let" means "hinder," not, as it does today, "allow" (although the older meaning of the word still survives, for example, in tennis, where a "let serve" is one that is hindered by the net on its way across). There are many words that can, like this, mislead us: "his" sometimes means "its," "an" often means "if," "envy" means something more like "malice," "cousin" means more generally "kinsman," and there are others, though all are easily defined. The difficulty is that we may not stop to look thinking we already know what the word means, but in this edition a ° following the word alerts a reader that there is a gloss in the left margin, and quickly readers get used to these older meanings.

Then, of course, there is the intimidation factor—strange, polysyllabic, or Latinate words that not only are foreign to us but also must have sounded strange even to Shakespeare's audiences. When Macbeth wonders whether all the water in all the oceans of the world will be able to clean his bloody hands after the murder of Duncan, he concludes: "No; this my hand will rather / The multitudinous seas incarnadine, / Making the green one red" (2.2.64–66). Duncan's blood staining Macbeth's murderous hand is so offensive that, not merely does it resist being washed off in water, but it will "the multitudinous seas incarnadine": that is, turn the sea-green oceans blood-red. Notes will easily clarify the meaning of the two odd words, but it is worth observing that they would have been as odd to Shakespeare's readers as they are to us. The *Oxford English Dictionary* (*OED*) shows no use of "multitudinous" before this, and it records no use of "incarnadine" before 1591 (*Macbeth* was written about 1606). Both are new words, coined from the Latin, part of a process in Shakespeare's time where English adopted many Latinate words as a mark of its own emergence as an important vernacular language. Here they are used to express the magnitude of Macbeth's offense, a crime not only against the civil law but also against the cosmic order, and then the simple monosyllables of turning "the green one red" provide an immediate (and needed) paraphrase and register his own sickening awareness of the true hideousness of his deed.

As with "multitudinous" in *Macbeth*, Shakespeare is the source of a great many words in English. Sometimes he coined them himself, or, if he didn't invent them, he was the first person whose writing of them has survived. Some of these words have become part of our language, so common that it is hard to imagine they were not always part of it: for example, "assassination" (*Macbeth*, 1.7.2), "bedroom" (*A Midsummer Night's Dream*, 2.2.57), "countless" (*Titus Andronicus*, 5.3.59), "fashionable" (*Troilus and Cressida*, 3.3.165), "frugal" (*The Merry Wives of Windsor*, 2.1.28), "laughable" (*The Merchant of Venice*, 1.1.56), "lonely" (*Coriolanus*, 4.1.30), and "useful" (*King John*, 5.2.81). But other words that he originated were not as, to use yet another Shakespearean coinage, "successful" (*Titus Andronicus*, 1.1.66). Words like "crimeless" (*Henry VI, Part Two*, 2.4.63, meaning "innocent"), "facinorous" (*All's Well That Ends Well*, 2.3.30, meaning "extremely wicked"), and "recountment" (*As You Like It*, 4.3.141, meaning "narrative" or "account") have, without much resistance, slipped into oblivion. Clearly Shakespeare liked words, even unwieldy ones. His working vocabulary, about 18,000 words, is staggering, larger than almost any other English writer, and he seems to be the first person to use in print about

1,000 of these. Whether he coined the new words himself or was intrigued by the new words he heard in the streets of London doesn't really matter; the point is that he was remarkably alert to and engaged with a dynamic language that was expanding in response to England's own expanding contact with the world around it.

But it is neither new words nor old ones that are the source of the greatest difficulty of Shakespeare's language. The real difficulty (and the real delight) comes in trying to see how he uses the words, how he endows them with more than their denotative meanings. Why, for example, does Macbeth say that he hopes that the "sure and firm-set earth" (2.1.56) will not hear his steps as he goes forward to murder Duncan? Here "sure" and "firm-set" mean virtually the same thing: stable, secure, fixed. Why use two words? If this were a student paper, no doubt the teacher would circle one of them and write "redundant." But the redundancy is exactly what Shakespeare wants. One word would do if the purpose were to describe the solidity of the earth, but here the redundancy points to something different. It reveals something about Macbeth's mind, betraying through the doubling how deep is his awareness of the world of stable values that the terrible act he is about to commit must unsettle.

Shakespeare's words usually work this way: in part describing what the characters see and as often betraying what they feel. The example from *Macbeth* is a simple example of how this works. Shakespeare's words are carefully patterned. How one says something is every bit as important as what is said, and the conspicuous patterns that are created alert us to the fact that something more than the words' lexical sense has been put into play. Words can be coupled, as in the example above, or knit into even denser metaphorical constellations to reveal something about the speaker (which often the speaker does not know), as in Prince Hal's promise to his father that he will outdo the rebels' hero, Henry Percy (Hotspur):

Percy is but my factor, good my lord,

To engross up glorious deeds on my behalf.

And I will call him to so strict account

That he shall render every glory up,

Yea, even the slightest worship of his time,

Or I will tear the reckoning from his heart.

(Henry IV, Part One, 3.2.147–152)

The Prince expresses his confidence that he will defeat Hotspur, but revealingly in a reiterated language of commercial exchange ("factor," "engross," "account," "render," "reckoning") that tells us something important both about the Prince and the ways in which he understands his world. In a play filled with references to coins and counterfeiting, the speech demonstrates not only that Hal has committed himself to the business at hand, repudiating his earlier, irresponsible tavern self, but also that he knows it is a business rather than a glorious world of chivalric achievement; he inhabits a world in which value (political as well as economic) is not intrinsic but determined by what people are willing to invest, and he proves himself a master of producing desire for what he has to offer.

Or sometimes it is not the network of imagery but the very syntax that speaks, as when Claudius announces his marriage to Hamlet's mother:

Therefore our sometime sister, now our Queen,

Th' imperial jointress to this warlike state,

Have we—as 'twere with a defeated joy,

With an auspicious and a dropping eye,

With mirth in funeral and with dole in marriage,

In equal scale weighing delight and dole—

Taken to wife.   *(Hamlet, 1.2.8–14)*

All he really wants to say here is that he has married Gertrude, his former sister-in-law: "Therefore our sometime sister . . . Have we . . . Taken to wife." But the straightforward sentence gets interrupted and complicated, revealing his own discomfort with the announcement. His elaborations and intensifications of Gertrude's role ("sometime sister," "Queen," "imperial jointress"), the self-conscious rhetorical balancing of the middle three lines (indeed "in equal scale weighing delight and dole"), all declare by the all-too obvious artifice how desperate he is to hide the awkward facts behind a veneer of normalcy and propriety. The very unnaturalness of the sentence is what alerts us that we are meant to understand more than the simple relation of fact.

Why doesn't Shakespeare just say what he means? Well, he does—exactly what he means. In the example from *Hamlet* just above, Shakespeare shows us something about Claudius that Claudius doesn't know himself. Always Shakespeare's words will offer us an immediate sense of what is happening, allowing us to follow the action, but they also offer us a counterplot, pointing us to what might be behind the action, confirming or contradicting what the characters say. It is a language that shimmers with promise and possibility, opening the characters' hearts and minds to our view—and all we have to do is learn to pay attention to what is there before us.

Shakespeare's Verse

Another distinctive feature of Shakespeare's dramatic language is that much of it is in verse. Almost all of the plays mix poetry and prose, but the poetry dominates. *The Merry Wives of Windsor* has the lowest percentage (only about 13 percent verse), while *Richard II* and *King John* are written entirely in verse (the only examples, although *Henry VI, Part One* and *Part Three* have only a very few prose lines). In most of the plays, about 70 percent of the lines are written in verse.

Shakespeare's characteristic verse line is a non-rhyming iambic pentameter ("blank verse"), ten syllables with every second one stressed. In *A Midsummer Night's Dream*, Titania comes to her senses after a magic potion has led her to fall in love with an ass-headed Bottom: "Methought I was enamored of an ass" (4.1.76). Similarly, in *Romeo and Juliet*, Romeo gazes up at Juliet's window: "But soft, what light through yonder window breaks" (2.2.2). In both these examples, the line has ten syllables organized into five regular beats (each beat consisting of the stress on the second syllable of a pair, as in "But soft," the da-dum rhythm forming an "iamb"). Still, we don't hear these lines as jingles; they seem natural enough, in large part because this dominant pattern is varied in the surrounding lines.

The play of stresses indeed becomes another key to meaning, as Shakespeare alerts us to what is important. In *Measure for Measure*, Lucio urges Isabella to plead for her brother's life: "Oh, to him, to him, wench! He will relent" (2.2.129). The iambic norm (unstressed-stressed) tells us (and an actor) that the emphasis at the beginning of the line is on "to" not "him"—it is the action not the object that is being emphasized—and at the end of the line the stress falls on "will." Alternatively, the line can play against the established norm. In *Hamlet*, Claudius corrects Polonius's idea of what is bothering the Prince: "Love? His affections do not that way tend" (3.1.161). The iambic norm forces the emphasis onto "that" ("do not *that* way tend"), while the syntax forces an unexpected stress on the opening word, "Love." In the famous line, "The course of true love never did run smooth" (*A Midsummer Night's Dream*, 1.1.134), the iambic expectation is varied in both the middle and at the end of the line. Both "love" and the first syllable of "never" are stressed, as are both syllables at the end: "run smooth," creating a metrical foot in which both syllables are stressed (called a "spondee"). The point to notice is that the "da-dum, da-dum, da-dum, da-dum, da-dum" line is not inevitable; it merely sets an expectation against which many variations can be heard.

In fact, even the ten-syllable norm can be varied. Shakespeare sometimes writes lines with fewer or more syllables. Often there is an extra, unstressed syllable at the end of a line (a so-called "feminine ending"); sometimes there are verse lines with only nine. In *Henry IV, Part One*, King Henry replies incredulously to the rebel Worcester's claim that he hadn't "sought" the confrontation with the King: "You have not sought it. How comes it then?" (5.1.27). There are only nine syllables here (some earlier editors, seeking to "correct" the verse, added the word "sir" after the first question to regularize the line). But the pause where one expects a stressed syllable is dramatically effective, allowing the King's anger to be powerfully present in the silence.

As even these few examples show, Shakespeare's verse is unusually flexible, allowing a range of rhythmical effects. It should not be understood as a set of strict rules but as a flexible set of practices rooted in dramatic necessity. It is designed to highlight ideas and emotions, and it is based less upon rigid syllable counts than on an arrangement of stresses within an understood temporal norm, as one might expect from a poetry written to be heard in the theater rather than read on the page.

Here Follows Prose

Although the plays are dominated by verse, prose plays a significant role. Shakespeare's prose has its own rhythms, but it lacks the formal patterning of verse, and so is printed without line breaks and without the capitals that mark the beginning of a verse line. Like many of his fellow dramatists, Shakespeare tended to use prose for comic scenes, the shift from verse serving, especially in his early plays, as a social marker. Upper-class characters speak in verse; lower-class characters speak in prose. Thus, in *A Midsummer Night's Dream*, the Athenians of the court, as well as the fairies, all speak in verse, but the "rude mechanicals," Bottom and his artisan friends, all speak in prose, except for the comic verse they speak in their performance of "Pyramis and Thisbe."

As Shakespeare grew in experience, he became more flexible about the shifts from verse to prose, letting it, among other things, mark genre rather than class and measure various kinds of intensity. Prose becomes in the main the medium of comedy. The great comedies, like *Much Ado About Nothing*, *Twelfth Night*, and *As You Like It*, are all more than 50 percent prose. But even in comedy, shifts between verse and prose may be used to measure subtle emotional changes. In Act One, scene three of *The Merchant of Venice*, Shylock and Bassanio begin the scene speaking of matters of business in prose, but when Antonio enters and the deep conflict between the Christian and the Jew becomes evident, the scene shifts to verse. But prose may itself serve in moments of emotional intensity. Shylock's famous speech in Act Three, scene one, "Hath not a Jew eyes . . ." is all in prose, as is Hamlet's expression of disgust at the world ("I have of late—but wherefore I know not—lost all my mirth . . .") at 3.1.261–276. Shakespeare comes to use prose to vary the tone of a scene, as the shift from verse subtly alerts an audience or a reader to some new emotional register.

Prose becomes, as Shakespeare's art matures, not inevitably the mark of the lower classes but the mark of a salutary daily-ness. It is appropriately the medium in which letters are written, and it is the medium of a common sense that will at least challenge the potential self-deceptions of grandiloquent speech. When Rosalind mocks the excesses and artifice of Orlando's wooing in Act Four, scene one of *As You Like It*, it is in prose that she seeks something genuine in the expression of love:

The poor world is almost six thousand years old, and in all this time there was not any man died in his own person, *videlicit* [i.e., namely], in a love cause. . . . Men have died from time to time, and worms have eaten them, but not for love.

Here the prose becomes the sound of common sense, an effective foil to the affectation of pinning poems to trees and thinking that it is real love.

It is not that prose is artless; Shakespeare's prose is no less self-conscious than his verse. The artfulness of his prose is different, of course. The seeming ordinariness of his prose is no less an effect of his artistry than is the more obvious patterning of his verse. Prose is no less serious, compressed, or indeed figurative. As with his verse, Shakespeare's prose performs numerous tasks and displays various, subtle formal qualities; and recognizing the possibilities of what it can achieve is still another way of seeing what Shakespeare puts right before us to show us what he has hidden.

Further Reading

N. F. Blake, *Shakespeare's Language: An Introduction* (New York: St. Martin's Press, 1983).

Jonathan Hope, *Shakespeare's Grammar* (London: Thomson, 2003).

Sister Miriam Joseph, *Shakespeare's Use of the Arts of Language* (New York: Columbia University Press, 1947).

M. M. Mahood, *Shakespeare's Wordplay* (London: Methuen, 1957).

Russ McDonald, *Shakespeare and the Arts of Language* (Oxford: Oxford University Press, 2001).

Brian Vickers, *The Artistry of Shakespeare's Prose* (London: Methuen, 1968).

George T. Wright, *Shakespeare's Metrical Art* (Berkeley: Univ. of California Press, 1991).

Key to the Play Text

Symbols

°	Indicates an explanation or definition in the left-hand margin.
¹	Indicates a gloss on the page facing the play text.
[]	Indicates something added or changed by the editors (i.e., not in the early printed text that this edition of the play is based on).

Terms

Q1, First Quarto An edition of the play printed in 1600, and the basis for this edition (see Editing *A Midsummer Night's Dream*, page 235).

Q2, Second Quarto An edition of the play printed in 1619.

F, Folio, or *First Folio* The first collected edition of Shakespeare's plays, printed in 1623.

A Midsummer Night's Dream

William Shakespeare

List of Roles

Theseus	*Duke of Athens*
Hippolyta	*Queen of the Amazons, to wed Theseus*
Philostrate	*Master of Revels*
Egeus	*Athenian lord and father of Hermia*
Hermia	*daughter of Egeus, in love with Lysander*
Lysander	*in love with Hermia*
Demetrius	*in love with Hermia and favored by Egeus*
Helena	*in love with Demetrius*
Oberon	*King of the Fairies*
Titania	*Queen of the Fairies*
Robin Goodfellow	*a mischievous fairy (or puck), Oberon's attendant*
Peaseblossom	
Cobweb	
Mote	*fairies attending Titania*
Mustardseed	
Peter **Quince**	*a carpenter, playing Prologue*
Nick **Bottom**	*a weaver, playing Pyramus*
Francis **Flute**	*a bellows-mender, playing Thisbe*
Tom **Snout**	*a tinker, playing Wall*
Snug	*a joiner, playing Lion*
Robin **Starveling**	*a tailor, playing Moonshine*

Lords, attendants, and fairies

1   *how slow / This old moon wanes. She*
    lingers my desires, / Like to a stepdame
    or a dowager / Long withering out a
    young man's revenue

    Impatient for his wedding night,
    Theseus compares the slowly
    waning moon to an old widow
    who retains possession of her
    late husband's estate, thus
    thwarting her son's desire to
    collect his inheritance. Just as the
    young man will receive his *reve-*
    nue upon the old widow's death,
    so Theseus will receive his bride
    once the old moon has waned
    away and a new moon shines.
    Through inheritance of marital
    property and independence from a
    husband's control, a widow in
    Renaissance England could enjoy
    an unusual degree of autonomy for
    a woman. The familiar cultural
    stereotype of widows as lusty
    manipulators of young men was a
    response to the perceived threat of
    their social and economic power.
    Since Theseus is about to marry an
    Amazon (see note 2), the epitome
    of female independence and
    strength, it is significant that he
    alludes disapprovingly to a
    widow's power over a young man.
    However, the play also provides an
    alternative, more positive, view of
    the widow. Whereas Theseus
    imagines an old widow wasting
    away with age while she wastes
    away her son's inheritance,

    Lysander assures Hermia that his
    generous widow aunt will help him
    fulfill his romantic desires (1.1.157–
    160).

2   *like to a silver bow / Now bent in Heaven*

    Hippolyta imagines the crescent of
    the moon as Diana's silver hunting
    bow. Diana was the Roman goddess
    of the hunt, of chastity, and of the
    moon. The Amazons—a tribe of
    mythical women warriors, of whom
    Hippolyta was queen—worshipped
    her as their primary deity. (See
    Longer Note on page 231.)

3   *The pale companion is not for our pomp*

    I.e., melancholy is not suitable for
    our celebrations

4   *wooed thee with my sword / And won*
    thy love doing thee injuries

    Theseus claimed Hippolyta as his
    bride when he conquered the
    Amazons.

5   **Lysander** and **Demetrius**

    In the Quarto, the entry direction
    reads "*and* Lysander *and* Helena,
    and Demetrius." Helena, however,
    is not required until her marked
    entrance at line 179.

Act 1, Scene 1

*Enter **Theseus**, **Hippolyta**, [and **Philostrate**,] with others.*

Theseus

Now, fair Hippolyta, our nuptial hour

quickly Draws on apace.° Four happy days bring in

Another moon. But, oh, methinks how slow

delays This old moon wanes. She lingers° my desires,

Like to a stepdame or a dowager   5

Long withering out a young man's revenue. [1]

Hippolyta

absorb Four days will quickly steep° themselves in night;

Four nights will quickly dream away the time,

And then the moon, like to a silver bow

Now bent in Heaven, [2] shall behold the night   10

festivities Of our solemnities.°

Theseus

            Go, Philostrate;

Stir up the Athenian youth to merriments.

lively Awake the pert° and nimble spirit of mirth;

Turn melancholy forth to funerals:

The pale companion is not for our pomp. [3]   15

                   [**Philostrate** *exits.*]

Hippolyta, I wooed thee with my sword

And won thy love doing thee injuries. [4]

But I will wed thee in another key:

public celebration With pomp, with triumph,° and with reveling.

*Enter **Egeus** and his daughter **Hermia**, and **Lysander***
*and **Demetrius**. [5]*

Egeus

Happy be Theseus, our renownèd Duke.   20

1 *the bosom of my child*

My child's heart

2 *sung / With feigning voice verses of feigning love, / And stol'n the impression of her fantasy*

Sung in a soft voice songs of false love, and captivated her imagination. *Impression* refers to a figure stamped in wax; Egeus literally accuses Lysander of stamping his own image onto Hermia's impressionable mind.

3 *messengers / Of strong prevailment in unhardened youth*

I.e., items that can powerfully influence innocent youth

4 *Be it so*

If it turns out that

Theseus

Thanks, good Egeus. What's the news with thee?

Egeus

anger Full of vexation° come I with complaint

Against my child, my daughter Hermia.

—Stand forth, Demetrius.—My noble lord,

This man hath my consent to marry her.   25

—Stand forth, Lysander.—And, my gracious Duke,

This man hath bewitched the bosom of my child. [1]

—Thou, thou, Lysander, thou hast given her rhymes

And interchanged love tokens with my child.

Thou hast by moonlight at her window sung   30

With feigning voice verses of feigning love,

And stol'n the impression of her fantasy [2]

trinkets / decorative items With bracelets of thy hair, rings, gauds,° conceits,°

Knickknacks Knacks,° trifles, nosegays, sweetmeats—messengers

Of strong prevailment in unhardened youth. [3]   35

stolen With cunning hast thou filched° my daughter's heart,

Turned her obedience (which is due to me)

To stubborn harshness.—And, my gracious Duke,

Be it so [4] she will not here before your Grace

Consent to marry with Demetrius,   40

I beg the ancient privilege of Athens:

As she is mine, I may dispose of her—

Which shall be either to this gentleman

Or to her death—according to our law

enacted Immediately provided° in that case.   45

Theseus

What say you, Hermia? Be advised, fair maid:

To you your father should be as a god,

created One that composed° your beauties, yea, and one

To whom you are but as a form in wax,

By him imprinted and within his power   50

1   *To you your father should be as a god, / One that composed your beauties, yea, and one / To whom you are but as a form in wax, / By him imprinted and within his power / To leave the figure or disfigure it*

In *A Midsummer Night's Dream*, as in most Shakespearean comedies, there are no mothers, only fathers. But in this speech the erasure of the mother goes even further. Theseus depicts Egeus as a godlike artist or writer who has singularly *composed* Hermia and thus has the right to *disfigure* his creation. The metaphor of biological conception as an *imprint[ing]*, as of a seal on soft wax, goes back to the ancient Greek philosophers Plato and Aristotle. In *Of Generation*, Aristotle describes semen as the "active" force that imprints a form on the "passive" raw material of the uterus: this imprinted form becomes the fetus. Through this metaphor of imprinting, Theseus gives Egeus all the credit for Hermia's creation. Nonetheless, Egeus's complaint that Lysander has *stol'n the impression* of Hermia's *fantasy* (1.1.32) reveals limits to the father's power over his daughter's body. Egeus is angry that Lysander has stolen Hermia's heart not only from Demetrius but from himself.

2   *livery*

Uniform (here, referring specifically to a nun's habit)

3   *mewed*

Caged (a *mew* being a cage for keeping hawks)

4   *barren sister*

Chaste nun

5   *You can endure the livery of a nun, / For aye to be in shady cloister mewed / To live a barren sister all your life, / Chanting faint hymns to the cold, fruitless moon*

(See LONGER NOTE on page 232.)

6   *earthlier happy is the rose distilled*

The rose that is plucked and distilled (to make perfume) is happier during its time on the earth than the rose that is allowed to wither. Theseus argues that while chaste nuns may be *thrice-blessed* in Heaven, women who give in to their sexuality are happier during their mortal lives.

To leave the figure or disfigure it. [1]
Demetrius is a worthy gentleman.

Hermia

So is Lysander.

Theseus

                           In himself he is,

lacking / approval   But in this kind, wanting° your father's voice,°
The other must be held the worthier.   55

Hermia

I would my father looked but with my eyes.

Theseus

Rather your eyes must with his judgment look.

Hermia

I do entreat your Grace to pardon me.
I know not by what power I am made bold,

reflect on   Nor how it may concern° my modesty   60
In such a presence here to plead my thoughts,
But I beseech your Grace that I may know
The worst that may befall me in this case
If I refuse to wed Demetrius.

Theseus

Either to die the death or to abjure   65
Forever the society of men.
Therefore, fair Hermia, question your desires,

i.e., emotions   Know of your youth, examine well your blood,°
Whether, if you yield not to your father's choice,
You can endure the livery [2] of a nun,   70

ever   For aye° to be in shady cloister mewed [3]
To live a barren sister [4] all your life,
Chanting faint hymns to the cold, fruitless moon. [5]

control / passions   Thrice-blessèd they that master° so their blood°
To undergo such maiden pilgrimage,   75
But earthlier happy is the rose distilled [6]

1   *my virgin patent*

    I.e., my right to remain a virgin

2   *unwishèd yoke*

    Unwanted authority

3   *he would*

    I.e., your father wishes

4   *crazèd title*

    **Flawed claim (*crazed* means both
    literally "cracked" and figuratively
    "insane")**

5   *Do you marry him.*

    **I.e. you marry him (*do* was often
    used this way for emphasis, rather
    than to pose a question)**

6   *As well possessed*

    I.e., with equal wealth

7   *My fortunes every way as fairly ranked, /
    If not with vantage*

    **My fortunes are equal to his in
    every way, if not better.**

Than that which, withering on the virgin thorn,
Grows, lives, and dies in single blessedness.

Hermia

So will I grow, so live, so die, my lord,
Before Ere° I will yield my virgin patent¹ up   80
Unto his Lordship, whose unwishèd yoke²
My soul consents not to give sovereignty.

Theseus

Take time to pause, and by the next new moon—
i.e., wedding The sealing° day betwixt my love and me
For everlasting bond of fellowship—   85
Upon that day either prepare to die
For disobedience to your father's will,
Or else to wed Demetrius, as he would,³
vow Or on Diana's altar to protest°
ever For aye° austerity and single life.   90

Demetrius

Relent, sweet Hermia—and, Lysander, yield
Thy crazèd title⁴ to my certain right.

Lysander

You have her father's love, Demetrius.
Let me have Hermia's. Do you marry him.⁵

Egeus

Scornful Lysander, true, he hath my love,   95
And what is mine my love shall render him,
And she is mine, and all my right of her
assign I do estate° unto Demetrius.

Lysander

descended [*to* **Theseus**] I am, my lord, as well derived° as he,
As well possessed.⁶ My love is more than his,   100
My fortunes every way as fairly ranked,
If not with vantage,⁷ as Demetrius'.
And, which is more than all these boasts can be,

1   *Made love to*

    Courted

2   *spotted and inconstant*

    Tarnished and unfaithful

3   *overfull of self-affairs*

    **Preoccupied with my own
    concerns**

4   *What cheer*

    **I.e., how do you feel? Hippolyta
    has said nothing since her first
    speech, but this line may indicate
    that she has reacted in some way to
    Hermia's dilemma.**

5   *Of something nearly that concerns
    yourselves*

    **About something that closely
    concerns both of you**

6   *How chance*

    How comes it that

I am beloved of beauteous Hermia.

insist upon   Why should not I then prosecute° my right?   105

swear / face   Demetrius—I'll avouch° it to his head°—

Made love to[1] Nedar's daughter, Helena,

And won her soul. And she, sweet lady, dotes,

Devoutly dotes, dotes in idolatry

Upon this spotted and inconstant[2] man.   110

Theseus

I must confess that I have heard so much

And with Demetrius thought to have spoke thereof,

But being overfull of self-affairs,[3]

My mind did lose it.—But, Demetrius, come;

And come, Egeus. You shall go with me.   115

instruction   I have some private schooling° for you both.

As for / prepare   —For° you, fair Hermia, look you arm° yourself

To fit your fancies to your father's will,

Or else the law of Athens yields you up

make less severe   (Which by no means we may extenuate°)   120

To death or to a vow of single life.

—Come, my Hippolyta. What cheer,[4] my love?

—Demetrius and Egeus, go along.

I must employ you in some business

In preparation for   Against° our nuptial and confer with you   125

Of something nearly that concerns yourselves.[5]

Egeus

With duty and desire we follow you.

All exit [except **Lysander** *and* **Hermia**].

Lysander

How now, my love? Why is your cheek so pale?

How chance[6] the roses there do fade so fast?

Hermia

Probably / lack   Belike° for want° of rain, which I could well   130

Provide   Beteem° them from the tempest of my eyes.

1   *For aught*

    According to everything

2   *different in blood*

    Mismatched in social status

3   *stood upon the choice of friends*

    **Depended on the decision of
    relatives**

4   *a sympathy in choice*

    I.e., love that is reciprocated

5   *That in a spleen unfolds both Heaven and
    Earth*

    **That, in a fit of rage, reveals both
    Heaven and Earth (the *spleen* was
    thought to be the source of sudden
    outbursts of anger)**

6   *So quick bright things come to confusion*

    **In such a manner do vital (*quick*),
    splendid creatures come to their
    ruin.**

7   *It stands as an edict in destiny*

    **It is an inevitable law concerning
    the destiny of lovers (i.e., that they
    will always encounter obstacles)**

8   *let us teach our trial patience*

    **Let us learn to be patient in the
    face of this difficulty**

Lysander

Ay me! For aught[1] that I could ever read,

Could ever hear by tale or history,

The course of true love never did run smooth,

But either it was different in blood[2]—   135

Hermia

obstacle / (in status)   O cross!° Too high° to be enthralled to low.

Lysander

mismatched   Or else misgraftèd° in respect of years—

Hermia

O spite! Too old to be engaged to young.

Lysander

Or else it stood upon the choice of friends[3]—

Hermia

O Hell, to choose love by another's eyes!   140

Lysander

Or, if there were a sympathy in choice,[4]

War, death, or sickness did lay siege to it,

momentary   Making it momentany° as a sound,

Swift as a shadow, short as any dream,

coal-black   Brief as the lightning in the collied° night   145

That in a spleen unfolds both Heaven and Earth,[5]

before   And ere° a man hath power to say "Behold!"

The jaws of darkness do devour it up:

So quick bright things come to confusion.[6]

Hermia

always   If then true lovers have been ever° crossed,   150

It stands as an edict in destiny.[7]

Then let us teach our trial patience,[8]

Because it is a customary cross,

As due to love as thoughts and dreams and sighs,

love's   Wishes and tears, poor fancy's° followers.   155

1   *remote seven leagues*

Seven leagues away (a league is a unit of distance measuring about 3 miles)

2   *To do observance to a morn of May*

A legacy of pagan agricultural festivals, "rites of May" were celebrations of fertility performed throughout early summer in England. Contemporary accounts of May Day celebrations describe London citizens feasting in the meadows and woods outside the city, setting up maypoles, dancing, performing plays, and lighting bonfires. Some Protestant reformers condemned May games for their association with Catholic feast days and for the sexual license they supposedly encouraged. The Purtian polemicist Philip Stubbes recounts with horror how May Day revelers, inspired by Satan, dance around the maypole as if they were pagans worshiping an idol. Stubbes also claims that the majority of young women who spend the night reveling in the woods lose their virginity before daybreak. Although Shakespeare's young pagan lovers become involved in erotic intrigues when they flee into the forest, they nonetheless emerge with their sexual purity and intentions to marry still intact.

3   *his best arrow with the golden head*

In Ovid's *Metamorphoses* (Book I), Cupid is said to have two kinds of arrows: arrows with heads of gold and arrows with heads of lead. The *golden* arrows made people fall in love, while the lead arrows made people fall out of love.

4   *simplicity of Venus' doves*

Innocence of Venus's doves. Venus was Cupid's mother and the Roman goddess of love, and she traveled in a chariot drawn by doves.

5   *by that fire which burned the Carthage Queen / When the false Trojan under sail was seen*

The *Carthage Queen* is Dido, whose suicide by fire is recounted by the Roman poet Virgil in *The Aeneid*. A survivor of the Trojan War, Aeneas lands in Carthage, where Dido takes him in as her lover, but he abandons her in order to fulfill his destiny as founder of the Roman Empire. Betrayed by the *false Trojan*, Dido throws herself on a pyre. Swearing an oath by Dido's *fire*, Hermia conveys the depth of her commitment to Lysander—she, too, faces the choice of dying for love—but she thereby evokes a story of male infidelity and betrayal.

6   *Whither away?*

Where are you going?

Lysander

argument A good persuasion.° Therefore hear me, Hermia.

I have a widow aunt, a dowager

Of great revenue, and she hath no child.

From Athens is her house remote seven leagues, [1]

regards And she respects° me as her only son.   160

There, gentle Hermia, may I marry thee,

And to that place the sharp Athenian law

Cannot pursue us. If thou lov'st me, then

away from Steal forth° thy father's house tomorrow night,

beyond And in the wood, a league without° the town,   165

Where I did meet thee once with Helena

To do observance to a morn of May, [2]

There will I stay for thee.

Hermia

                              My good Lysander,

I swear to thee by Cupid's strongest bow,

By his best arrow with the golden head, [3]   170

By the simplicity of Venus' doves, [4]

By that which knitteth souls and prospers loves,

And by that fire which burned the Carthage Queen

When the false Trojan under sail was seen, [5]

By all the vows that ever men have broke   175

(In number more than ever women spoke),

In that same place thou hast appointed me,

Tomorrow truly will I meet with thee.

Lysander

Keep promise, love. Look, here comes Helena.

Enter **Helena**.

Hermia

God speed, fair Helena! Whither away? [6]   180

1   *Demetrius loves your fair.*

Demetrius loves your kind of beauty (not mine).

2   *lodestars*

Stars used by sailors for navigation

3   *your tongue's sweet air*

I.e., the music of your speech

4   *favor*

Both "appearance" and "approval"; Helena wants to *catch* both Hermia's looks and the attention those looks get from Demetrius.

5   *Were the world mine, Demetrius being bated, / The rest I'd give to be to you translated.*

If I owned the whole world except for Demetrius, I'd give it all up to be transformed into you.

Helena

Call you me "fair"? That "fair" again unsay.

fortunate   Demetrius loves your fair.[1] O happy° fair!

Your eyes are lodestars,[2] and your tongue's sweet air[3]

melodious   More tunable° than lark to shepherd's ear

When wheat is green, when hawthorn buds appear.   185

contagious   Sickness is catching.° Oh, were favor[4] so,

Yours would I catch, fair Hermia, ere I go.

My ear should catch your voice. My eye, your eye.

My tongue should catch your tongue's sweet melody.

Were the world mine, Demetrius being bated,   190

The rest I'd give to be to you translated.[5]

Oh, teach me how you look and with what art

influence   You sway° the motion of Demetrius' heart.

Hermia

I frown upon him, yet he loves me still.

Helena

Oh, that your frowns would teach my smiles such skill!   195

Hermia

I give him curses, yet he gives me love.

Helena

Oh, that my prayers could such affection move!

Hermia

The more I hate, the more he follows me.

Helena

The more I love, the more he hateth me.

Hermia

His folly, Helena, is no fault of mine.   200

Helena

None but your beauty. Would that fault were mine!

Hermia

Take comfort. He no more shall see my face.

Lysander and myself will fly this place.

1   *what graces in my love do dwell, / That he hath turned a Heaven unto a Hell*

How much beauty and grace is in Lysander, that he is able to turn what once seemed perfect into something detestable.

2   *Phoebe*

Alternate name for Diana, the goddess of the moon. Here Lysander uses the name *Phoebe* to refer to the moon itself.

3   *Emptying our bosoms of their counsel swelled*

The Quarto and Folio read "emptying our bosoms of their counsel sweld" (i.e., "swelled"). Modern editors usually emend "swelled" to "sweet," since "sweet" rhymes with "meet" in the next line. Emended to "counsel sweet," the line refers to the innocent sharing of anything on their minds. In the reading of early texts, however, "swelled" must modify "bosoms," and Hermia thus appears to refer to the girls' habit of pouring out to each other the weighty confidences that filled their hearts. Although the original reading of "sweld" interrupts the pattern of rhyming couplets in the speech (*I/lie, sweld/meet*, etc.), that interruption can be taken to foreshadow the sundering of the women's friendship in the forest. When Hermia arranges to meet Lysander on the same flower banks where she and Helena used to lie, she already anticipates the obsolescence of that same-sex friendship as her primary emotional relationship. Moreover, the image of *swelled* bosoms conveys an intense physical and emotional intimacy consistent with Shakespeare's depictions of girlhood friendship in plays such as *As You Like It* (1599) and *The Two Noble Kinsmen* (1613–1614), a play drawing on the same Chaucerian source as *A Midsummer Night's Dream*. In *The Two Noble Kinsmen*, Emilia, the unmarried sister of Hippolyta, recalls her childhood friendship with a girl named Flavinia. Deeply infatuated with each other, the girls did everything alike: if Emilia placed a flower between her breasts, "then but beginning / To swell about the blossom," Flavinia would do the same (1.3.67–68).

4   *stranger companies*

the company of strangers

5   *We must starve our sight / From lovers' food*

I.e., we must refrain from seeing each other

6   *How happy some o'er other some can be!*

How much happier some people can be than some others.

7   *He will not know what all but he do know*

He refuses to acknowledge what everyone else knows (i.e., that Helena is just as attractive as Hermia)

Before the time I did Lysander see
Seemed Athens as a paradise to me. 205
Oh, then, what graces in my love do dwell,
That he hath turned a Heaven unto a Hell! [1]

Lysander

Helen, to you our minds we will unfold.
Tomorrow night when Phoebe[2] doth behold

face / mirror Her silver visage° in the wat'ry glass,° 210
Decking with liquid pearl the bladed grass

always (A time that lovers' flights doth still° conceal),
Through Athens' gates have we devised to steal.

Hermia

(*to* **Helena**) And in the wood where often you and I

pale / accustomed Upon faint° primrose beds were wont° to lie, 215
Emptying our bosoms of their counsel swelled, [3]
There my Lysander and myself shall meet;
And thence from Athens turn away our eyes
To seek new friends and stranger companies. [4]
Farewell, sweet playfellow. Pray thou for us, 220
And good luck grant thee thy Demetrius!

your word —Keep word,° Lysander. We must starve our sight
From lovers' food[5] till morrow deep midnight.

                                    Hermia *exits.*

Lysander

I will, my Hermia. Helena, adieu.
As you on him, Demetrius dote on you! **Lysander** *exits.* 225

Helena

How happy some o'er other some can be! [6]
Through Athens I am thought as fair as she.
But what of that? Demetrius thinks not so.
He will not know what all but he do know, [7]
And as he errs, doting on Hermia's eyes, 230

1 *holding no quantity*

Out of all proportion (to their actual worth)

2 *of any judgment taste*

Any inkling of good judgment

3 *As waggish boys in game themselves forswear*

As mischievous boys will lie when playing a game

4 *So he dissolved, and showers of oaths did melt*

He disappeared along with his promises (of love)

5 *it is a dear expense*

(1) it will cost me dearly (because Demetrius will then be able to follow Hermia); (2) he will think even thanking me is galling; (3) even his grudging thanks will be welcome and valuable to me

So I, admiring of his qualities.
Things base and vile, holding no quantity, [1]
Love can transpose to form and dignity.
Love looks not with the eyes but with the mind,
And therefore is winged Cupid painted blind.   235
Nor hath Love's mind of any judgment taste; [2]
symbolize / reckless Wings and no eyes figure° unheedy° haste,
And therefore is Love said to be a child,
misled Because in choice he is so oft beguiled.°
As waggish boys in game themselves forswear, [3]   240
So the boy Love is perjured everywhere.
eyes (archaic) For ere Demetrius looked on Hermia's eyne°
He hailed down oaths that he was only mine;
And when this hail some heat from Hermia felt,
So he dissolved, and showers of oaths did melt. [4]   245
I will go tell him of fair Hermia's flight;
Then to the wood will he tomorrow night
information Pursue her. And for this intelligence,°
If I have thanks it is a dear expense. [5]
But herein mean I to enrich my pain,   250
To have his sight thither and back again.   *She exits.*

1 *joiner*

Furniture maker

2 *generally*

**Bottom confuses *generally* with
"individually"; he will make similar
mistakes throughout this scene.**

3 *scrip*

**Often glossed "script," the
theatrical sense is, however,
unknown before the late 19th
century; *scrip* means a piece of
paper, usually with writing on it.**

4 *treats on*

Takes as its subject

5 *grow to a point*

Reach a conclusion

6 *Marry*

**A common, mild oath; a
contraction of *By the Virgin Mary***

Act 1, Scene 2

Enter **Quince** *the carpenter, and* **Snug** *the joiner,* [1] *and* **Bottom**
the weaver, and **Flute** *the bellows-mender, and* **Snout** *the tinker,*
and **Starveling** *the tailor.*

Quince
Is all our company here?

Bottom
You were best to call them generally, [2] man by man,
according to the scrip. [3]

Quince
Here is the scroll of every man's name which is thought

play fit, through all Athens, to play in our interlude° before   5
the Duke and the Duchess on his wedding day at night.

Bottom
First, good Peter Quince, say what the play treats on, [4]
then read the names of the actors, and so grow to a
point. [5]

Quince
Marry, [6] our play is *The Most Lamentable Comedy and Most*   10
Cruel Death of Pyramus and Thisbe.

Bottom
A very good piece of work, I assure you, and a merry.
Now, good Peter Quince, call forth your actors by the
scroll.—Masters, spread yourselves.

Quince
Answer as I call you.—Nick Bottom, the weaver?   15

Bottom
Ready. Name what part I am for and proceed.

Quince
You, Nick Bottom, are set down for Pyramus.

Bottom
What is Pyramus? A lover or a tyrant?

1   *I will condole in some measure.*

     I will grieve in an appropriate
     manner.

2   *my chief humor is for a tyrant. I could*
     play Ercles rarely

     I.e., what I most want to play is a
     tyrant; I could play Hercules
     magnificently. Shakespeare is
     poking fun at a bombastic
     tradition of acting that stretches
     back to the religious drama of the
     Middle Ages. Performed by
     artisans on important Christian
     feast days, these plays depicted
     villains, such as King Herod, as
     ranting tyrants. Bottom refers
     more directly to the roaring
     Hercules (*Ercles*) in Thomas
     Studley's translation (1581) of
     Seneca's *Hercules Oetaeus*, whose
     heroism was, as Robert Greene
     said, "terribly thundered on the
     stage" (1592; see *Ercles' vein* in line
     34).

3   *a part to tear a cat in, to make all split*

     I.e., part that would let me rant and
     rave, to bring down the house

4   *Phibbus' car*

     I.e., the chariot of Phoebus Apollo
     (the Roman sun god). The spelling
     may be intended to reflect
     Bottom's mispronunciation.

Quince

gallantly A lover that kills himself most gallant° for love.

Bottom

require That will ask° some tears in the true performing of it. If   20
I do it, let the audience look to their eyes. I will move
storms. I will condole in some measure. [1] To the
inclination rest.—Yet my chief humor° is for a tyrant. I could play
i.e, Hercules Ercles° rarely, [2] or a part to tear a cat in, to make all split. [3]

> The raging rocks   25
> And shivering shocks
> Shall break the locks
> Of prison gates.
> And Phibbus' car [4]
> Shall shine from far   30
> And make and mar
> The foolish Fates.

This was lofty!—Now name the rest of the players.
style —This is Ercles' vein,° a tyrant's vein. A lover is more
mournful condoling.°   35

Quince

Francis Flute, the bellows-mender?

Flute

Here, Peter Quince.

Quince

Flute, you must take Thisbe on you.

Flute

What is Thisbe? A wandering knight?

Quince

It is the lady that Pyramus must love.   40

Flute

Nay, faith, let not me play a woman. I have a beard
coming.

1   *That's all one.*

That doesn't matter.

2   *Thisne*

Perhaps intended as a pet name for
Thisbe, or Bottom's conception of
how the name *Thisbe* might sound
when spoken in Pyramus's voice,
or merely a characteristic error.

Quince

That's all one. [1] You shall play it in a mask, and you may

high-pitched / like speak as small° as you will.°

Bottom

If An° I may hide my face, let me play Thisbe too! I'll   45

monstrously speak in a monstrous° little voice: "Thisne, [2] Thisne!"
—"Ah, Pyramus, my lover dear, thy Thisbe dear and
lady dear!"

Quince

No, no. You must play Pyramus.—And Flute, you Thisbe.

Bottom

Well, proceed.   50

Quince

Robin Starveling, the tailor?

Starveling

Here, Peter Quince.

Quince

Robin Starveling, you must play Thisbe's mother.
—Tom Snout, the tinker?

Snout

Here, Peter Quince.   55

Quince

You, Pyramus' father.—Myself, Thisbe's father.—Snug
the joiner, you, the lion's part.—And I hope here is a

appropriately cast play fitted.°

Snug

Have you the lion's part written? Pray you, if it be, give
it me, for I am slow of study.   60

Quince

extemporaneously You may do it extempore,° for it is nothing but roaring.

Bottom

so that Let me play the lion too. I will roar, that° I will do any
man's heart good to hear me. I will roar that I will make

1   *An you should do it too terribly, you would
    fright the Duchess and the ladies that they
    would shriek—and that were enough to
    hang us all.*

The actors' anxieties reveal that
theater could be a risky business in
spite of its opportunities for
considerable financial success. The
actors in *A Midsummer Night's Dream* are
amateurs, but they believe that the
Duke will reward their performance
with a lifetime pension of *sixpence a day*
(4.2.17), though nowhere does the
Duke confirm such an arrangement.
Nonetheless, while they anticipate
some recompense from the Duke,
Bottom and his associates never forget
the dangers of a theatrical confrontation with royalty. So literally do they
take the power of theatrical representation that they believe that an actor
in a lion suit might terrify female
spectators, an offense they fear
would be punished by hanging.
The artisans are still haunted by
anxiety during their first rehearsal in
the forest, when they decide that
Snug must introduce himself through
the hole in the neck of the lion's suit
and that a prologue must explain that
the actor playing Pyramus does not
actually kill himself. In Shakespeare's
London, actors and playwrights were
not hanged, but could be fined and
jailed, for performing satirical scenes
that offended the powerful, and
indeed Shakespeare's company was

tried (though acquitted) by the Star
Chamber in 1601, when it was thought
that their performance of *Richard II* was
intended to support the failed
rebellion by the Earl of Essex. Before
every play could be performed it had to
be approved by the Master of the
Revels, a court appointed officer who
also chose which plays were to be
honored with performances at court.
Theseus seems to employ Philostrate
in a similar position, describing him as
our usual manager of mirth (5.1.35).

2   *sucking dove*

Bottom confuses two images of
mildness: a *sitting dove* (a dove on a
nest) and a *sucking lamb* (a lamb that
has not yet been weaned)

3   *you must needs*

You need to

4   *French crown-color*

I.e., golden (the color of a *French
crown,* or a gold coin)

5   *Some of your French crowns have no hair
    at all, and then you will play barefaced.*

Quince puns on Bottom's image of
French crown-color beard, alluding to
the hair loss that was a common
symptom of syphilis, known as the
"French disease."

6   *parts*

Scripts, though see 3.1.88 and
note.

the Duke say, "Let him roar again. Let him roar again."

Quince

If   An° you should do it too terribly, you would fright the   65
Duchess and the ladies that they would shriek—and
that were enough to hang us all. [1]

All

That would hang us, every mother's son.

Bottom

I grant you, friends, if you should fright the ladies out
choice   of their wits, they would have no more discretion° but   70
i.e., moderate   to hang us. But I will aggravate° my voice so that I will
for you   roar you° as gently as any sucking dove. [2] I will roar you
as if   an° 't were any nightingale.

Quince

You can play no part but Pyramus, for Pyramus is a
handsome   sweet-faced man, a proper° man as one shall see in a   75
summer's day, a most lovely, gentlemanlike man;
Therefore you must needs [3] play Pyramus.

Bottom

Well, I will undertake it. What beard were I best to play
it in?

Quince

Why, what you will.   80

Bottom

perform   I will discharge° it in either your straw-color beard,
tan / dyed deep red   your orange-tawny° beard, your purple-in-grain° beard, or
your French crown-color [4] beard, your perfect yellow.

Quince

heads   Some of your French crowns° have no hair at all, and
then you will play barefaced. [5]—But masters, here are   85
your parts. [6] And I am to entreat you, request you, and
learn   desire you to con° them by tomorrow night and meet
outside   me in the palace wood, a mile without° the town, by

1   *bill of properties*

   List of props

2   *obscenely*

   Bottom probably merely mistakes
   obscenely for "seemly," though his
   word has an unintended propriety,
   as etymologically it means "away
   from the public eye."

3   *Hold or cut bowstrings.*

   I.e., keep your promise (to meet) or
   quit now, like the modern "fish or
   cut bait." The phrase *cut bowstrings*
   may refer to the tradition that
   English archers, when defeated in
   battle, would cut their own
   bowstrings so that their weapons
   would be of no use to their enemies.

moonlight. There will we rehearse, for if we meet in
the city we shall be dogged with company, and our   90
intentions devices° known. In the meantime I will draw a bill of
properties¹ such as our play wants. I pray you, fail me not.

Bottom

We will meet, and there we may rehearse most
obscenely² and courageously. Take pains. Be perfect.
Adieu.   95

Quince

At the Duke's oak we meet.

Bottom

Enough. Hold or cut bowstrings.³   *They exit.*

1   *Over park, over pale*

A *park* was a tract of land held by royal grant usually reserved for hunting; a *pale* was any fenced-in area.

2   *the moon's sphere*

According to Ptolemaic astronomy, the moon was fixed in a transparent globe that revolved around the Earth.

3   *dew her orbs upon the green*

I.e., adorn the meadow with her fairy rings (circles of matted grass thought to be caused by dancing fairies)

4   *cowslips*

Wild plants with clusters of fragrant yellow flowers that radiate from their central stalk.

5   *In those freckles live their savors.*

I.e., the ruby spots on the flowers are the source of their sweet scent

6   *lob*

Oafish lout or bumpkin; the use of the word perhaps suggests that Robin (like Oberon) was played by an adult actor instead of by one of the boys in the acting company who most likely played the other fairies.

7   *keep his revels*

Hold his festivities

8   *Oberon*

The Fairy King Oberon appears in several works with which Shakespeare might have been familiar, such as the romance *Duke Huon of Bourdeaux* (translated into English 1533–1542), Edmund Spenser's epic poem *The Faerie Queene* (1590), and Robert Greene's play *James IV* (1591).

9   *passing fell and wrath*

Extremely fierce and angry

10 *A lovely boy stolen from an Indian king. / She never had so sweet a changeling*

Fairies were often thought to steal human children from their cradles and leave fairy children in their place. The changeling boy has no lines and might or might not appear on stage. Shakespeare's use of *changeling* for the son stolen from the Indian King is anomalous, since the term generally connoted not the stolen mortal child but the undesirable fairy child left in its place. It is not clear how the Indian boy came to be in Titania's possession. Whereas Robin claims that Titania stole the boy from the Indian King, Titania explains that she adopted him for the sake of his mother, her devoted votaress (2.1.135–137).

Act 2, Scene 1

Enter a **Fairy** *at one door and* **Robin** *Goodfellow at another.*

Robin

To where   How now, spirit? Whither° wander you?

Fairy

Over hill, over dale,

Through   Thorough° bush, thorough brier,

Over park, over pale,[1]

Thorough flood, thorough fire,   5

I do wander everywhere

Swifter than the moon's sphere,[2]

And I serve the Fairy Queen

To dew her orbs upon the green.[3]

bodyguards   The cowslips[4] tall her pensioners° be.   10

In their gold coats spots you see.

gifts   Those be rubies, fairy favors.°

In those freckles live their savors.[5]

I must go seek some dewdrops here

And hang a pearl in every cowslip's ear.   15

Farewell, thou lob[6] of spirits. I'll be gone.

soon   Our Queen and all her elves come here anon.°

Robin

The King doth keep his revels[7] here tonight.

Take heed the Queen come not within his sight.

For Oberon[8] is passing fell and wrath,[9]   20

to serve as   Because that she as° her attendant hath

A lovely boy stolen from an Indian king.

She never had so sweet a changeling,[10]

And jealous Oberon would have the child

roam   Knight of his train, to trace° the forests wild.   25

by force   But she perforce° withholds the lovèd boy,

1   *all her joy*

The focus of her happiness

2   *spangled starlight sheen*

The flickering starlight

3   *Robin Goodfellow*

Although tradition usually names him "Puck," a *puck* is a particular type of roguish spirit (see line 40), and Robin Goodfellow is the name Shakespeare gives him, taking it from English folklore. Traditionally, Robin Goodfellow was thought to perform the kind of pranks described in this scene. Shakespeare, however, also associates Robin with more malevolent figures such as the *hobgoblin* and the *Goblin* who is *feared in field and town* (2.1.40; 3.2.398–399). In the late 16th century, belief in fairies and magic was generally in decline. Like Theseus expressing his disbelief in *antique fables* and *fairy toys* (5.1.3), Reginald Scot, author of *The Discovery of Witchcraft* (1584), argues that Robin Goodfellow and hobgoblins were nothing but old wives' tales meant to frighten children.

4   *Skim milk, and sometimes labor in the quern*

Steal the cream from the top of the milk and sometimes interfere with the grinding of grain. A *quern* was a small grinder used to make flour.

5   *bear no barm*

Form no head; i.e., Robin prevents the ale from fermenting properly and forming a frothy head.

6   *You do their work, and they shall have good luck*

In addition to causing mischief, Robin would also do housework and bring good luck to people who showed him respect.

7   *Neighing in likeness of a filly foal*

I.e., Robin tricks the stallion by neighing like a young mare.

8   *a gossip's bowl*

A gossipy woman's drinking mug

9   *crab*

Crab apple (which was sometimes floated in a hot drink)

10   *dewlap*

Leathery flap of skin on the neck

11   *Tailor*

It was common to cry "Tailor!" when suddenly falling backward. It is unclear how the custom started, perhaps because tailors sat on the floor to alter clothing, or because *tail* was slang for "buttocks."

Crowns him with flowers, and makes him all her joy. [1]

i.e., Titania and Oberon And now they° never meet in grove or green,

spring By fountain° clear or spangled starlight sheen, [2]

argue / so that But they do square,° that° all their elves for fear 30

themselves Creep into acorn cups and hide them° there.

Fairy

physique Either I mistake your shape and making° quite,

mischievous / rascally Or else you are that shrewd° and knavish° sprite

Called Robin Goodfellow. [3] Are not you he

village population That frights the maidens of the villagery,° 35

Skim milk, and sometimes labor in the quern, [4]

uselessly And bootless° make the breathless housewife churn,

And sometime make the drink to bear no barm, [5]

Mislead night-wanderers, laughing at their harm?

Those that "hobgoblin" call you, and "sweet puck," 40

You do their work, and they shall have good luck. [6]

Are not you he?

Robin

correctly Thou speak'st aright.°

I am that merry wanderer of the night.

I jest to Oberon and make him smile

trick When I a fat and bean-fed horse beguile,° 45

Neighing in likeness of a filly foal. [7]

And sometime lurk I in a gossip's bowl [8]

In very likeness of a roasted crab, [9]

And when she drinks, against her lips I bob

And on her withered dewlap [10] pour the ale. 50

The wisest aunt telling the saddest tale

three-footed Sometime for three-foot° stool mistaketh me;

Then slip I from her bum, down topples she,

And "Tailor!" [11] cries, and falls into a cough,

assembly of people And then the whole quire° hold their hips and laugh, 55

increase / sneeze And waxen° in their mirth, and neeze,° and swear

1   *Ill met*

A mark of Oberon's anger; "well met" would be the customary greeting

2   *Titania*

Various connections can be drawn between Titania and Queen Elizabeth. The figure of a Fairy Queen was sometimes included in courtly entertainments presented to Queen Elizabeth, and the title figure of Edmund Spenser's epic poem *The Faerie Queen* (1590) overtly complements the Queen. The name *Titania* comes from Ovid's *Metamorphoses*, where it designates various female figures identified as "Titaness" or "Titan's daughter." Titans were ancient Greek gods of the generation preceding the Olympian gods led by Zeus.

3   *wanton*

A rebellious, stubborn person, (but also a promiscuous woman)

4   *Corin*

In Elizabeth pastoral literature, *Corin* and *Phillida* (line 68) were conventional names for a lovesick shepherd and his beloved shepherdess. Titania is accusing Oberon of wasting his time writing poems and seducing women, thereby ignoring his royal responsibilities in Fairyland.

5   *pipes of corn*

A wind instrument made of grain stalks (*corn* referred to any cereal plant)

6   *versing love*

Speaking love poems

7   *farthest step*

Utmost limit

8   *buskined*

Wearing knee-high hunting boots

9   *Glance at my credit with Hippolyta*

I.e., disparage my honor by bringing up Hippolyta

A merrier hour was never wasted there.

i.e., make room   But, room,° fairy! Here comes Oberon.

Fairy

And here my mistress. Would that he were gone!

*Enter [***Oberon***,] the King of Fairies, at one door with his*
*train, and [***Titania***,] the Queen, at another, with hers.*

Oberon

Ill met[1] by moonlight, proud Titania.[2]   60

Titania

What, jealous Oberon?—Fairies, skip hence.

sworn to give up   I have forsworn° his bed and company.

Oberon

Wait   Tarry,° rash wanton.[3] Am not I thy lord?

Titania

Then I must be thy lady, but I know

When thou hast stol'n away from Fairyland,   65

And in the shape of Corin[4] sat all day

Playing on pipes of corn[5] and versing love[6]

To amorous Phillida. Why art thou here,

Come from the farthest step[7] of India,

in truth   But that, forsooth,° the bouncing Amazon,   70

Your buskined[8] mistress and your warrior love,

To Theseus must be wedded, and you come

To give their bed joy and prosperity?

Oberon

How canst thou thus for shame, Titania,

Glance at my credit with Hippolyta,[9]   75

for   Knowing I know thy love to° Theseus?

Didst not thou lead him through the glimmering night

Away from / raped   From° Perigenia, whom he ravishèd?°

1 *Didst thou not lead him through the*
   glimmering night / From Perigenia,
   whom he ravishèd? / And make him
   with fair Aegles break his faith, / With
   Ariadne and Antiopa?
   (See LONGER NOTE on page 232.)

2 *middle summer's spring*
   Beginning of midsummer

3 *we*
   I.e., Titania and her attendant fairies

4 *By pavèd fountain, or by rushy brook*
   By clear springs with pebbly
   bottoms, or by streams with reeds
   along their banks

5 *ringlets*
   Circle dances

6 *brawls*
   Quarrels (but "brawl" was also the
   name for a raucous French dance)

7 *piping to us in vain*
   Whistling for us to no avail

8 *overborne their continents*
   Overflowed their banks

9 *lost his sweat*
   Wasted his effort

10 *ere his youth attained a beard*
    I.e., before it had a chance to mature

11 *the murrain flock*
    Sheep that had been killed by an
    infectious disease

12 *nine-men's-morris*
    A board game similar to checkers,
    in which the goal is to move the
    nine pegs into lines of threes, each
    of which cost the opponent one
    peg; often played outdoors on a
    board scratched into the dirt

13 *the quaint mazes in the wanton green /*
    For lack of tread are undistinguishable
    The elaborate mazes cut into the
    thick grass have grown over because
    they are no longer walked in

14 *rheumatic diseases*
    Respiratory sicknesses marked by
    discharge of rheum (mucus)

15 *distemperature*
    I.e., bad weather (imagined as
    caused by the moon's anger)

16 *old Hiems' thin and icy crown*
    Hiems **was a Roman personification**
    of winter, often pictured as an old
    man with a crown of ice on his
    balding head.

17 *odorous chaplet*
    Sweet-smelling bouquet

promise of fidelity	And make him with fair Aegles break his faith,°
	With Ariadne and Antiopa? [1]
	Titania
lies	These are the forgeries° of jealousy,
	And never, since the middle summer's spring, [2]
valley / meadow	Met we [3] on hill, in dale,° forest, or mead,°
	By pavèd fountain, or by rushy brook, [4]
shoreline	Or in the beachèd margent° of the sea,
to the sound of	To dance our ringlets [5] to° the whistling wind,
	But with thy brawls [6] thou hast disturbed our sport.
	Therefore the winds, piping to us in vain, [7]
	As in revenge have sucked up from the sea
i.e., falling as rain	Contagious fogs, which falling° in the land
paltry	Have every pelting° river made so proud
	That they have overborne their continents. [8]
pulled	The ox hath therefore stretched° his yoke in vain,
unripe	The ploughman lost his sweat, [9] and the green° corn
	Hath rotted ere his youth attained a beard. [10]
sheep pen	The fold° stands empty in the drownèd field,
	And crows are fatted with the murrain flock. [11]
	The nine-men's-morris [12] is filled up with mud,
elaborate	And the quaint° mazes in the wanton green
	For lack of tread are undistinguishable. [13]
lack	The human mortals want° their winter cheer.
	No night is now with hymn or carol blessed;
	Therefore the moon, the governess of floods,
i.e., dampens	Pale in her anger, washes° all the air,
So that	That° rheumatic diseases [14] do abound.
through	And thorough° this distemperature [15] we see
white-headed	The seasons alter: hoary-headed° frosts
	Fall in the fresh lap of the crimson rose,
	And on old Hiems' thin and icy crown [16]
	An odorous chaplet [17] of sweet summer buds

Line numbers: 80, 85, 90, 95, 100, 105, 110

1　*wonted liveries*

　Customary dress

2　*Therefore the winds, piping to us in vain, / As in revenge have sucked up from the sea / Contagious fogs. . . . The spring, the summer, / The childing autumn, angry winter change / Their wonted liveries, and the mazèd world, / By their increase, now knows not which is which.*

　Because of the bizarre weather patterns, the *mazèd* (bewildered) *world* can no longer tell what season it is. Titania's extensive description of disruptions in nature might have reminded Shakespeare's audience of the terrible weather and failed harvests that caused widespread hardship for the poor in England during the mid-1590s. In 1595, the scarcity and high price of food provoked rioting by London apprentices, young men training for professions such as those represented by the plays' artisans.

3　*Do you amend*

　You must fix

4　*The Fairyland buys not the child of me.*

　All of Fairyland would not be enough to buy the child from me.

5　*votress*

　A woman who has vowed to serve a particular god or goddess

6　*Neptune's yellow sands*

　***Neptune* was the Roman god of the sea.**

7　*Marking th' embarkèd traders on the flood*

　Watching the merchant ships setting out to sea

8　*we have laughed to see the sails conceive / And grow big-bellied with the wanton wind*

　Titania and her votress are amused by the sight of the ships' sails, which billow outward as though the *wanton* (amorous) *wind* has impregnated them.

9　*swimming gait*

　Movement as if sailing on the waves

10　*of that boy did die*

　Died in childbirth giving birth to him

Is, as in mockery, set. The spring, the summer,

fruitful   The childing° autumn, angry winter change

bewildered   Their wonted liveries, [1] and the mazèd° world,

By their increase, now knows not which is which. [2]

offspring   And this same progeny° of evils comes   115

From our debate, from our dissension.

origin   We are their parents and original.°

Oberon

Do you amend [3] it then. It lies in you.

Why should Titania cross her Oberon?

I do but beg a little changeling boy   120

page   To be my henchman.°

Titania

                  Set your heart at rest.

The Fairyland buys not the child of me. [4]

His mother was a votress [5] of my order,

And in the spicèd Indian air by night

Full often hath she gossiped by my side,   125

And sat with me on Neptune's yellow sands, [6]

Marking th' embarkèd traders on the flood, [7]

When we have laughed to see the sails conceive

And grow big-bellied with the wanton wind, [8]

Which she, with pretty and with swimming gait [9]   130

Imitating   Following°—her womb then rich with my young

        squire—

Would imitate and sail upon the land

trinkets   To fetch me trifles° and return again,

As from a voyage, rich with merchandise.

But she, being mortal, of that boy did die, [10]   135

And for her sake do I rear up her boy,

And for her sake I will not part with him.

Oberon

to stay   How long within this wood intend you stay?°

1   *spare your haunts*

   Avoid your territory

2   *chide downright*

   Openly fight

3   *Thou shalt not from this grove*

   You will not leave this grove

4   *shot madly from their spheres*

   Flew wildly out of their orbits

5   *a fair vestal thronèd by the west*

   A beautiful virgin, ruling in the west. Oberon's story about a virgin monarch who could not be hit by Cupid's arrow almost certainly refers to Queen Elizabeth, known as the Virgin Queen because of her refusal to marry and her pledge to remain chaste (See "Introduction to *A Midsummer Night's Dream*," pages 3–4).

6   *As it should*

   As if it could

7   *wat'ry moon*

   The moon was often called *wat'ry* (watery) because of its effect on the tides.

Titania

Perhaps Perchance° till after Theseus' wedding day.

circle dance If you will patiently dance in our round°   140

And see our moonlight revels, go with us.

If not, shun me, and I will spare your haunts. [1]

Oberon

Give me that boy, and I will go with thee.

Titania

Not for thy fairy kingdom.—Fairies, away!

We shall chide downright [2] if I longer stay.   145

                         [**Titania** *and her train*] *exit.*

Oberon

Well, go thy way. Thou shalt not from this grove [3]

insult Till I torment thee for this injury.°

[*to* **Robin**] My gentle puck, come hither. Thou

      rememb'rest

When Since° once I sat upon a promontory

And heard a mermaid on a dolphin's back   150

sweet / sound Uttering such dulcet° and harmonious breath°

That the rude sea grew civil at her song,

And certain stars shot madly from their spheres [4]

To hear the seamaid's music?

Robin

                              I remember.

Oberon

That very time I saw (but thou couldst not)   155

Flying between the cold moon and the Earth,

fully Cupid all° armed. A certain aim he took

At a fair vestal thronèd by the west [5]

arrow And loosed his love shaft° smartly from his bow

As it should [6] pierce a hundred thousand hearts.   160

could But I might° see young Cupid's fiery shaft

Quenched in the chaste beams of the wat'ry moon, [7]

1   *imperial votress*

    See line 158 and note.

2   *love-in-idleness*

    I.e., the wild pansy

3   *leviathan*

    A huge sea creature mentioned in the
    Bible (see Psalm 104:26 and Job 41),
    thought by many to be a whale

4   *league*

    A unit of length, roughly
    equivalent to three miles

5   *put a girdle*

    Circle; circumnavigate

6   *Having once*

    Once I have

And the imperial votress[1] passèd on
In maiden meditation, fancy-free.

noted   Yet marked° I where the bolt of Cupid fell.   165
It fell upon a little western flower,
Before milk-white, now purple with love's wound,
And maidens call it "love-in-idleness."[2]
Fetch me that flower. The herb I showed thee once.
The juice of it on sleeping eyelids laid   170

either   Will make or° man or woman madly dote
Upon the next live creature that it sees.
Fetch me this herb and be thou here again
Ere the leviathan[3] can swim a league.[4]

Robin

I'll put a girdle[5] round about the Earth   175
In forty minutes.   [**Robin** *exits.*]

Oberon

Having once[6] this juice,
I'll watch Titania when she is asleep
And drop the liquor of it in her eyes.
The next thing then she, waking, looks upon   180
(Be it on lion, bear, or wolf, or bull,
On meddling monkey or on busy ape)

essence   She shall pursue it with the soul° of love.
And ere I take this charm from off her sight
(As I can take it with another herb)   185
I'll make her render up her page to me.
But who comes here? I am invisible,

conversation   And I will overhear their conference.°

Enter **Demetrius**, **Helena** *following him.*

Demetrius

I love thee not, therefore pursue me not.

1　*The one I'll stay, the other stayeth me.*

I.e., one of them (Lysander) I'll stop, the other (Hermia) stops me (by transfixing me with her beauty, or perhaps by stopping my heart). Modern editors often amend the reading (found both in the Quarto and Folio) to "The one I'll slay, the other slayeth me." The emended reading is not impossible ("t" and "l" can be easily confused in manuscript), and the reading anticipates the physical and emotional violence the play associates with frustrated desire.

2　*were stol'n unto*

Had fled into

3　*Leave you*

Abandon

4　*speak you fair*

Speak lovingly to you

5　*give me leave*

Allow me

Where is Lysander and fair Hermia?   190
The one I'll stay, the other stayeth me. [1]
Thou told'st me they were stol'n unto [2] this wood.

frantic   And here am I, and wood° within this wood
Because I cannot meet my Hermia.
Hence, get thee gone and follow me no more.   195

Helena

a hard, magnetic stone   You draw me, you hard-hearted adamant,°
But yet you draw not iron, for my heart
Is true as steel. Leave you [3] your power to draw,
And I shall have no power to follow you.

Demetrius

Do I entice you? Do I speak you fair? [4]   200
Or rather do I not in plainest truth
Tell you I do not nor I cannot love you?

Helena

And even for that do I love you the more.
I am your spaniel, and, Demetrius,
The more you beat me, I will fawn on you.   205

merely   Use me but° as your spaniel—spurn me, strike me,
Neglect me, lose me. Only give me leave, [5]
Unworthy as I am, to follow you.

worse   What worser° place can I beg in your love
(And yet a place of high respect with me)   210
Than to be usèd as you use your dog?

Demetrius

Tempt not too much the hatred of my spirit,
For I am sick when I do look on thee.

Helena

And I am sick when I look not on you.

Demetrius

discredit   You do impeach° your modesty too much,   215
To leave the city and commit yourself

1   *Your virtue is my privilege.*

Your goodness is my guarantee of safety

2   *For that*

Because

3   *in my respect*

From my perspective

4   *the story shall be changed. / Apollo flies, and Daphne holds the chase.*

The myth of Apollo and Daphne appears in Ovid's *Metamorphoses* (Book 1), a major influence on this play. Chased by a lustful Apollo, the virgin nymph Daphne prayed for help and was turned into a laurel tree, which saved her from being raped. Helena complains that her pursuit of Demetrius inverts the usual situation in which the strong pursues the weak. Oberon alludes to the Daphne myth when he calls Helena a *nymph* and promises to transform the fleeing Demetrius: *Ere he do leave this grove / Thou shalt fly him, and he shall seek thy love* (246–247). At first glance, it appears that Oberon intends to help Helena achieve Demetrius. However, Oberon actually promises to transform this "inverted" scenario in which a woman chases a man to a more conventional scenario in which a man chases a woman. One might ask why Helena would pursue

a man, if she, like Daphne, feared being raped. Oberon later explains that the love juice will cause Demetrius to be *More fond on her than she upon her love* (2.1.268). Oberon's solution to Helena's problem thus retains the imbalance of desire between the lovers, simply shifting the burden of that imbalance so that the man will desire the woman more than she will desire him.

5   *griffin*

An imaginary creature with the head, wings, and forelegs of an eagle and the body and hind legs of a lion

6   *When cowardice pursues and valor flies*

I.e., when women (stereotypically weak and marked by *cowardice*) pursue men (stereotypically strong and demonstrating *valor*)

7   *do not believe / But I shall do thee mischief*

Do not believe otherwise than that I will do you harm

8   *set a scandal on my sex*

I.e., cause women to behave in dishonorable ways (by forcing them to become the wooers)

Into the hands of one that loves you not,

To trust the opportunity of night

deserted And the ill counsel of a desert° place

With the rich worth of your virginity.   220

Helena

Your virtue is my privilege.[1] For that[2]

It is not night when I do see your face,

Therefore I think I am not in the night,

Nor doth this wood lack worlds of company,

For you in my respect[3] are all the world.   225

Then how can it be said I am alone

When all the world is here to look on me?

Demetrius

thickets I'll run from thee and hide me in the brakes,°

And leave thee to the mercy of wild beasts.

Helena

The wildest hath not such a heart as you.   230

Run when you will, the story shall be changed.

Apollo flies, and Daphne holds the chase.[4]

doe The dove pursues the griffin;[5] the mild hind°

useless Makes speed to catch the tiger—bootless° speed,

When cowardice pursues and valor flies.[6]   235

Demetrius

stay to hear I will not stay° thy questions. Let me go.

Or if thou follow me, do not believe

But I shall do thee mischief[7] in the wood.

Helena

Ay, in the temple, in the town, the field

You do me mischief. Fie, Demetrius!   240

Your wrongs do set a scandal on my sex.[8]

We cannot fight for love as men may do.

We should be wooed and were not made to woo.

[**Demetrius** *exits.*]

1   *upon the hand*

I.e., by the hand

2   *oxlips*

Large hybrid flowers created by crossing cowslips with primroses

3   *woodbine*

Usually is honeysuckle, but see 4.1.41–42, where clearly it marks a different plant. In both places it must refer to some other climbing plant like bindweed.

4   *sweet musk-roses and with eglantine*

Musk-roses and *eglantine* are two types of wild rose.

5   *sometime of the night*

I.e., at some point each night (or perhaps merely "some evenings," though Oberon's certainty of finding her suggests the former)

6   *Weed*

Garment (i.e., the snakeskin)

I'll follow thee and make a Heaven of Hell,

To die upon the hand[1] I love so well.   [**Helena** *exits.*]   245

Oberon

Fare thee well, nymph. Ere he do leave this grove

run from   Thou shalt fly° him, and he shall seek thy love.

              Enter [**Robin**].

Hast thou the flower there? Welcome, wanderer.

Robin

Ay, there it is.

Oberon

I pray thee give it me. [*takes flower from* **Robin**]   250

I know a bank where the wild thyme blows,

Where oxlips[2] and the nodding violet grows,

Quite overcanopied with luscious woodbine,[3]

With sweet musk-roses and with eglantine.[4]

There sleeps Titania sometime of the night,[5]   255

Lulled in these flowers with dances and delight,

sheds   And there the snake throws° her enameled skin,

Weed[6] wide enough to wrap a fairy in;

And with the juice of this I'll streak her eyes

And make her full of hateful fantasies. [*gives* **Robin** *part*

   of the flower]   260

Take thou some of it and seek through this grove.

A sweet Athenian lady is in love

With a disdainful youth. Anoint his eyes,

sees   But do it when the next thing he espies°

May be the lady. Thou shalt know the man   265

By the Athenian garments he hath on.

Manage   Effect° it with some care, that he may prove

1   *More fond on her than she upon her love*

**More in love with her than she now
is with him**

More fond on her than she upon her love, [1]
And look thou meet me ere the first cock crow.

Robin

Fear not, my lord. Your servant shall do so. 270

They exit [separately].

1   *quaint*

    (1) small and dainty; (2) ingenious;
    skillful

2   *Newts and blindworms*

    Two harmless species of small
    lizard, which many Elizabethans
    believed to be poisonous

3   *Philomel*

    I.e., nightingale. Another figure from
    Ovid's *Metamorphoses* (Book 6),
    Philomela was raped by her brother-
    in-law, who cut out her tongue to
    prevent her from revealing his
    identity. She was later transformed
    into a nightingale. Philomela's
    suffering might be taken as a fully
    realized tragic version of what
    Oberon does to Titania by
    confounding her sensory perceptions
    and forcing her to love Bottom.

Act 2, Scene 2

*Enter **Titania**, Queen of Fairies, with her train.*

Titania

circle dance   Come; now a roundel° and a fairy song.

Then for the third part of a minute, hence:

grubs   Some to kill cankers° in the musk-rose buds,

bats / leathery   Some war with reremice° for their leathern° wings

To make my small elves coats, and some keep back   5

The clamorous owl that nightly hoots and wonders

At our quaint¹ spirits. Sing me now asleep.

duties   Then to your offices° and let me rest.

                              [*She lies down and*] **Fairies** *sing.*

First Fairy

forked   [*sings*] You spotted snakes with double° tongue,

Thorny hedgehogs, be not seen.   10

Newts and blindworms,² do no wrong.

Come not near our Fairy Queen.

Fairies

[*sing*] Philomel,³ with melody

Sing in our sweet lullaby.

Lulla, lulla, lullaby, lulla, lulla, lullaby.   15

Never let   Never° harm

Nor spell nor charm

near   Come our lovely lady nigh.°

So good night, with lullaby.

First Fairy

[*sings*] Weaving spiders, come not here;   20

Hence, you long-legged spinners, hence!

Beetles black, approach not near;

Worm nor snail, do no offense.

Fairies

[*sing*] Philomel, with melody

1   *In thy eye that shall appear*

Whatever shall appear to your sight

Sing in our sweet lullaby.   25
Lulla, lulla, lullaby, lulla, lulla, lullaby.
Never harm
Nor spell nor charm
Come our lovely lady nigh.
So good night with lullaby.   30

[*Titania* *sleeps.*]

Second Fairy
Hence, away! Now all is well.
a short distance off One aloof° stand sentinel.

[*All but* **Titania** *and one fairy exit.*]

Enter **Oberon**.

Oberon
[*squeezing flower on* **Titania***'s eyelids*] What thou see'st
    when thou dost wake,
Do it for thy true love take.
Love and languish for his sake.   35
lynx   Be it ounce° or cat or bear,
Leopard   Pard° or boar with bristled hair,
In thy eye that shall appear¹
When thou wak'st, it is thy dear.
Wake when some vile thing is near.   [**Oberon** *exits.*] 40

Enter **Lysander** *and* **Hermia**.

Lysander
Fair love, you faint with wand'ring in the wood,
truth   And to speak troth,° I have forgot our way.
We'll rest us, Hermia, if you think it good,
wait   And tarry° for the comfort of the day.

1   *Be it so*

    Let it be so

2   *Oh, take the sense, sweet, of my innocence.*

    **Understand, my darling, the innocent
    sense in which I meant my words.**

3   *Love takes the meaning in love's
    conference.*

    **I.e., in the conversation (*conference*)
    of lovers, the shared love makes it
    possible to understand what is
    meant.**

4   *For, lying so, Hermia, I do not lie*

    **Punning on *lie* meaning both "lie
    down" and "speak untruly"**

Hermia

Be it so, [1] Lysander. Find you out a bed,   45

For I upon this bank will rest my head.   [*lies down*]

Lysander

One turf shall serve as pillow for us both,

vow   One heart, one bed, two bosoms, and one troth.°

[*starts to lie down next to her*]

Hermia

Nay, good Lysander. For my sake, my dear,

Lie further off yet. Do not lie so near.   50

Lysander

Oh, take the sense, sweet, of my innocence. [2]

Love takes the meaning in love's conference. [3]

I mean that my heart unto yours is knit

So that but one heart we can make of it.

chained together   Two bosoms interchainèd° with an oath—   55

So, then, two bosoms and a single troth.

Then by your side no bed room me deny,

For, lying so, Hermia, I do not lie. [4]

Hermia

plays with words   Lysander riddles° very prettily.

curse   Now much beshrew° my manners and my pride   60

If Hermia meant to say Lysander lied.

But, gentle friend, for love and courtesy

Lie further off in human modesty.

Such separation as may well be said

Becomes a virtuous bachelor and a maid.   65

So far be distant; and good night, sweet friend.

Thy love ne'er alter till thy sweet life end!

Lysander

Amen, amen to that fair prayer, say I.

And then end life when I end loyalty.

1   *let love forbid / Sleep his seat on thy eyelid*

I.e., let passion prevent you from sleeping

Here is my bed. Sleep give thee all his rest.   70
[lies down away from her]

Hermia

With half that wish the wisher's eyes be pressed.
[**Hermia** and **Lysander** sleep.]

Enter [**Robin**].

Robin

Through the forest have I gone,

But Athenian found I none

test   On whose eyes I might approve°

This flower's force in stirring love.   75

[sees **Lysander** and **Hermia**] Night and silence! Who is
here?

Clothing   Weeds° of Athens he doth wear.

he who   This is he,° my master said,

Despisèd the Athenian maid.

And here the maiden, sleeping sound   80

On the dank and dirty ground.

dares   Pretty soul! She durst° not lie

Near this lack-love, this kill-courtesy.

Scornful person   [squeezes flower on **Lysander**'s eyelids] Churl,° upon thy
eyes I throw

own   All the power this charm doth owe.°   85

When thou wak'st, let love forbid

Sleep his seat on thy eyelid. [1]

So awake when I am gone,

For I must now to Oberon.   He exits.

Enter **Demetrius** and **Helena**, running.

1 *on thy peril*

   He threatens her to keep her from following.

2 *The more my prayer, the lesser is my grace.*

   The more I pray, the less my prayers are rewarded

3 *attractive*

   Having the power to attract

4 *Do, as a monster, fly my presence thus*

   Runs from me like this, as if I were a monster

5 *sphery eyne*

   Starry eyes

6 *Transparent*

   Transparent here means "radiant and luminous," as well as the more common "able to be seen through" and "lacking in deceit." In calling Helena *transparent*, Lysander expresses his admiration for her radiant skin, through which he claims he can see her heart, the organ metaphorically associated with love. Yet this reference to a transparent breast evokes an unsettling image of anatomical dissection that seems out of place in a comedy. In Shakespeare's tragedies from *Titus Andronicus* to *King Lear* the imagery of dissection symbolizes the violent rending of familial and social bonds. Lysander's word thus resonates with Helena's growing conviction that she is being deliberately tortured by her friends.

7 *Nature shows art*

   Nature demonstrates its skill (by making Helena seem transparent)

8 *What though*

   So what if

Helena

Stay, though thou kill me, sweet Demetrius.   90

Demetrius

order / away   I charge° thee hence,° and do not haunt me thus.

Helena

i.e., in the dark   O, wilt thou darkling° leave me? Do not so.

Demetrius

Stay, on thy peril.[1] I alone will go.   [*He exits.*]

Helena

infatuated; foolish   Oh, I am out of breath in this fond° chase.

The more my prayer, the lesser is my grace.[2]   95

Happy is Hermia, wheresoe'er she lies,

For she hath blessèd and attractive[3] eyes.

How came her eyes so bright? Not with salt tears.

If so, my eyes are oft'ner washed than hers.

No, no, I am as ugly as a bear,   100

For beasts that meet me run away for fear.

if   Therefore no marvel though° Demetrius

as if I were   Do, as° a monster, fly my presence thus.[4]

mirror   What wicked and dissembling glass° of mine

myself with   Made me compare with° Hermia's sphery eyne?[5]   105

[*sees* **Lysander**] But who is here? Lysander, on the ground?

Dead or asleep? I see no blood, no wound.

—Lysander, if you live, good sir, awake.

Lysander

[*waking*] And run through fire I will for thy sweet sake.

Transparent[6] Helena! Nature shows art[7]   110

That through thy bosom makes me see thy heart.

Where is Demetrius? Oh, how fit a word

Is that vile name to perish on my sword!

Helena

Do not say so, Lysander. Say not so.

What though[8] he love your Hermia? Lord, what though?   115

1 *Who will not change a raven for a dove?*
Lysander's question marks the first time that the play raises the possibility of a significant difference in physical appearance between Hermia (the black *raven*) and Helena (the white *dove*). No such difference in appearance is ever suggested to exist between the two men. Most likely, this reflects the size and coloring differences between the boy actors who originally played the two female parts. Nonetheless, Lysander's distinction between black raven and white dove might simply function metaphorically to indicate his altered perception of beauty, so we cannot be certain that Hermia actually has darker hair or skin than Helena. In Shakespeare's culture, blackness typically connoted ugliness, promiscuity, and baseness, whereas whiteness or fairness connoted beauty, chastity, and gentility. Once Lysander considers Hermia undesirable, therefore, he begins to insult her as an *Ethiope* and *tawny Tartar* (3.2.257, 263).

2 *ripe not to reason*
Am too immature to show good judgment

3 *touching now the point of human skill*
Reaching now the pinnacle of human ability (to reason)

4 *the marshal to my will*
The overseer of my desire

5 *love's richest book*
I.e., Helena's eyes

6 *Good troth*
In truth

7 *good sooth*
Indeed; to say truly

8 *true gentleness*
Genuine courtesy

Yet Hermia still loves you. Then be content.

Lysander

Content with Hermia? No. I do repent

The tedious minutes I with her have spent.

Not Hermia but Helena I love.

exchange   Who will not change° a raven for a dove? [1]   120

The will of man is by his reason swayed,

And reason says you are the worthier maid.

Things growing are not ripe until their season,

So I, being young, till now ripe not to reason. [2]

And touching now the point of human skill, [3]   125

Reason becomes the marshal to my will [4]

read   And leads me to your eyes, where I o'erlook°

Love's stories written in love's richest book. [5]

Helena

Why / biting   Wherefore° was I to this keen° mockery born?

When at your hands did I deserve this scorn?   130

Is 't not enough, is 't not enough, young man,

That I did never, no, nor never can,

Deserve a sweet look from Demetrius' eye,

mock   But you must flout° my insufficiency?

Good troth, [6] you do me wrong; good sooth, [7] you do,   135

In such disdainful manner me to woo.

By necessity   But fare you well. Perforce° I must confess

I thought you lord of more true gentleness. [8]

Oh, that a lady of one man refused

Should of another therefore be abused!   *She exits.*   140

Lysander

She sees not Hermia.—Hermia, sleep thou there

And never mayst thou come Lysander near,

overindulgence   For, as a surfeit° of the sweetest things

The deepest loathing to the stomach brings,

1   *the heresies that men do leave / Are*
     hated most of those they did deceive
     The heresies that men renounce
     are most hated by those who once
     believed in them.

2   *an if*
     If

3   *of all loves*
     I.e., in the name of all loves; for
     love's sake

Or, as the heresies that men do leave   145
Are hated most of those they did deceive, [1]
So thou, my surfeit and my heresy,
i.e., By Of° all be hated, but the most of me.
direct —And all my powers, address° your love and might
To honor Helen and to be her knight.   *He exits.* 150

Hermia

[*waking*] Help me, Lysander; help me! Do thy best
To pluck this crawling serpent from my breast!
Ay me, for pity! What a dream was here!
Lysander, look how I do quake with fear.
Methought a serpent ate my heart away,   155
attack And you sat smiling at his cruel prey.°
gone Lysander!—What, removed?°—Lysander, lord!
—What, out of hearing gone? No sound, no word?
—Alack, where are you? Speak, an if[2] you hear.
Speak, of all loves! [3] I swoon almost with fear.   160
near No? Then I well perceive you are not nigh.°
Either death or you I'll find immediately.

She exits [and **Titania** *remains asleep].*

1   *this hawthorn brake our tiring-house*

    **This hawthorn thicket will be our
    dressing room. *Tiring-house* is a
    shortened form of *attiring-house*,
    the area behind the stage in an
    Elizabethan theater where actors
    would change into and out of
    costumes.**

2   *do it in action*

    Perform the play

3   *By 'r lakin*

    **A contraction of *By our ladykin*, or
    "little lady" (i.e., By the Virgin
    Mary)**

4   *Put them out of fear*

    Reassure them

Act 3, Scene 1

[**Titania** *still sleeps.*] *Enter the clowns* [**Bottom**, **Quince**, **Flute**, **Snug**, **Snout**, *and* **Starveling**].

Bottom

i.e. here   Are we all met?°

Quince

Right on time   Pat,° pat. And here's a marvelous convenient place for
our rehearsal. This green plot shall be our stage, this
thicket   hawthorn brake° our tiring-house, [1] and we will
do it in action [2] as we will do it before the Duke.   5

Bottom

Peter Quince—

Quince

good fellow   What say'st thou, bully° Bottom?

Bottom

There are things in this comedy of Pyramus and Thisbe
that will never please. First, Pyramus must draw a
sword to kill himself, which the ladies cannot abide.   10
How answer you that?

Snout

perilous   By 'r lakin, [3] a parlous° fear.

Starveling

I believe we must leave the killing out, when all is
done.

Bottom

bit   Not a whit.° I have a device to make all well. Write me a   15
prologue and let the prologue seem to say we will do
no harm with our swords, and that Pyramus is not
killed indeed. And for the more better assurance, tell
them that I, Pyramus, am not Pyramus, but Bottom the
weaver. This will put them out of fear. [4]   20

1 *eight and six*

Alternating eight-syllable lines and six-syllable lines; the verse form, often called "fourteeners," most commonly used in ballads.

2 *my life for yours*

I.e., I would sacrifice my life to protect yours

3 *it were pity of my life*

It would be at the risk of my life.

Quince

Well. We will have such a prologue, and it shall be
written in eight and six.[1]

Bottom

No. Make it two more: let it be written in eight and eight.

Snout

afraid Will not the ladies be afeard° of the lion?

Starveling

I fear it, I promise you.   25

Bottom

Masters, you ought to consider with yourselves. To
bring in (God shield us!) a lion among ladies is a most
terrifying dreadful thing. For there is not a more fearful° wildfowl
than your lion living, and we ought to look to 't.

Snout

Therefore another prologue must tell he is not a lion.   30

Bottom

Nay, you must name his name, and half his face must
be seen through the lion's neck, and he himself must
i.e., "effect" speak through, saying thus—or to the same defect°—
"Ladies," or "Fair ladies," "I would wish you" or "I
would request you" or "I would entreat you not to fear,   35
not to tremble, my life for yours.[2] If you think I come
hither as a lion, it were pity of my life.[3] No. I am no
such thing: I am a man as other men are." And there
indeed let him name his name and tell them plainly he
is Snug the joiner.   40

Quince

Well. It shall be so. But there is two hard things: that is,
to bring the moonlight into a chamber, for, you know,
Pyramus and Thisbe meet by moonlight.

Snout

Doth the moon shine that night we play our play?

1   *a bush of thorns and a lantern*

    **Traditionally, two accessories of
    the man in the moon**

2   *disfigure*

    Quince means *figure* **(i.e., represent)**

3   *loam*

    **A mixture of clay, sand, and straw
    used for making bricks**

4   *roughcast*

    **Lime mixed with gravel, a common
    plaster used for walls**

5   *let him hold his fingers thus*

    **Bottom probably holds his fingers
    in a V shape.**

Bottom

A calendar, a calendar! Look in the almanac. Find out   45
moonshine; find out moonshine!

Quince

[*takes out a book*] Yes, it doth shine that night.

Bottom

window sash Why, then may you leave a casement° of the great
chamber window where we play open, and the moon
may shine in at the casement.   50

Quince

Ay. Or else one must come in with a bush of thorns and
a lantern, [1] and say he comes to disfigure, [2] or to
represent; perform present,° the person of Moonshine. Then there is
another thing: we must have a wall in the great cham-
ber, for Pyramus and Thisbe, says the story, did talk   55
through the chink of a wall.

Snout

You can never bring in a wall. What say you, Bottom?

Bottom

Some man or other must present Wall, and let him
have some plaster, or some loam, [3] or some roughcast [4]
about him to signify wall. Or let him hold his fingers   60
thus, [5] and through that cranny shall Pyramus and
Thisbe whisper.

Quince

If that may be, then all is well. Come; sit down, every
mother's son, and rehearse your parts.—Pyramus, you
begin. When you have spoken your speech, enter into   65
thicket that brake.°—And so everyone according to his cue.

Enter **Robin** [*unseen*].

1   *hempen homespuns*

    I.e., country bumpkins (judging by
    their *homespun* clothing made of
    coarse fabric made from hemp)

2   *a play toward*

    A play in preparation

3   *must you*

    You must

4   *bristly juvenile*

    Bearded young man (the Quarto's
    "brisky," i.e., energetic, is not
    impossible but is nowhere else
    used by Shakespeare, and misses
    the joke about the inappropriate
    casting of Bottom as the young
    lover Pyramus)

5   *jew*

    Here intended as a term of
    endearment, possibly merely as a
    play on a shortened form of
    "juvenile" or an error for "jewel"

Robin

[*aside*] What hempen homespuns ¹ have we swagg'ring
    here,
So near the cradle of the Fairy Queen?
What, a play toward? ² I'll be an auditor.
An actor too, perhaps, if I see cause.   70

Quince

Speak, Pyramus.—Thisbe, stand forth.

Bottom

[*as* **Pyramus**] Thisbe, the flowers of odious savors
    sweet—

Quince

"Odious?" "Odors!"

Bottom

                         —odors savors sweet,
So hath thy breath, my dearest Thisbe dear.
But hark, a voice! Stay thou but here awhile,   75
And by and by I will to thee appear.   *He exits.*

Robin

[*aside*] A stranger Pyramus than e'er played here.

                                      [*He exits.*]

Flute

Must I speak now?

Quince

Ay, marry, must you. ³ For you must understand he goes
merely but° to see a noise that he heard, and is to come again.   80

Flute

[*as* **Thisbe**] Most radiant Pyramus, most lily-white of hue,
wild rose bush Of color like the red rose on triumphant brier,°
also Most bristly juvenile ⁴ and eke° most lovely jew, ⁵
As true as truest horse that yet would never tire,
I'll meet thee, Pyramus, at Ninny's tomb.   85

1   *Ninus'*

In Ovid's *Metamorphoses* (Book 4), Pyramus and Thisbe meet at the tomb of Ninus, the legendary founder of the ancient city of Ninevah.

2   *You speak all your part at once, cues and all.*

When rehearsing a play, Elizabethan actors received a cue script that only had their respective lines written out, along with cues that indicated when they should begin speaking. The nervous and inexperienced Flute reads all his lines at once, along with the cue lines from Pyramus's speeches.

3   Enter **Bottom**, wearing an ass's head

There are two obvious classical analogues for Bottom's transformation into an ass. In Ovid's *Metamorphoses* (Book 11), Apollo gives King Midas ass's ears to punish him for preferring the rustic music of Pan to his own elegant music. In *The Golden Ass*, a novel by the ancient Roman writer Lucius Apuleius (translated into English in 1566), the narrator is transformed into an ass through sorcery. As an ass, Lucius travels with a band of robbers and has sexual encounters with women. At the end of the story the goddess Isis transforms Lucius back into his human shape. Titania and Bottom might or might not have a sexual encounter after she leads him to her bower at the end of this scene. While some readers find the relationship between the Fairy Queen and the ass-headed weaver touchingly innocent or raucously absurd, others see in it a transgressive sexual intimacy, especially considering that on Shakespeare's stage a boy most likely played Titania and an adult man played Bottom. In 16th-century England, bestiality (like pederasty) was a capital crime, and records survive of men who were sentenced to hang for both crimes. Bottom's transformation into an ass is also open to a more uplifting allegorical interpretation. Such an interpretation might be guided by the *Praise of Folly*, an important philosophical text by the early 16th-century humanist scholar Erasmus. Using the ass to represent the pervasiveness of human folly, the *Praise of Folly* paradoxically celebrates the figure of the "wise fool."

4   *about a round*

In a circular dance

5   *knavery of them*

Joke of theirs

Quince

"Ninus'[1] tomb," man. Why, you must not speak that
yet. That you answer to Pyramus. You speak all your
part at once, cues and all.[2]—Pyramus, enter. Your cue
is past. It is "never tire."

Flute

Oh. [*as* **Thisbe**] As true as truest horse that yet would
never tire.   90

[*Enter* **Bottom**, *wearing an ass's head,*[3] *and* **Robin**.]

Bottom

handsome / would be   [*as* **Pyramus**] If I were fair,° Thisbe, I were° only thine.

Quince

Oh, monstrous! Oh, strange! We are haunted! Pray,
masters! Fly, masters! Help!

[**Quince**, **Flute**, **Snug**, **Snout**, *and* **Starveling** *exit*.]

Robin

I'll follow you. I'll lead you about a round,[4]

thicket   Through bog, through bush, through brake,° through brier.   95
Sometime a horse I'll be, sometime a hound,
A hog, a headless bear, sometime a fire,
And neigh, and bark, and grunt, and roar, and burn,
Like horse, hound, hog, bear, fire, at every turn.

He exits.

Bottom

Why do they run away? This is a knavery of them[5] to   100
make me afeard.

Enter **Snout**.

Snout

O Bottom, thou art changed! What do I see on thee?

1 *You see an ass head of your own*
   I.e., you see your own idiotic
   behavior

2 *little quill*
   Soft, high song

3 *plainsong*
   A plain, simple melody (like the
   repeated *cuckoo* call of the *cuckoo*)

4 *Whose note full many a man doth mark*
   Whose song many men hear. The
   cuckoo's call was often said to be
   "cuckold," the insulting name for
   the husband of an unfaithful wife.
   Strangely enough, Oberon
   attempts to control his wife by
   putting her in a position to cuckold
   him with Bottom.

5 *And dares not answer "Nay"*
   I.e., and dares not deny that he is a
   cuckold (lest he be caught in a lie)

6 *who would set his wit to*
   I.e., who would bother
   acknowledging. From the proverb
   "Do not set your wit against a fool's."

7 *Who would give a bird the lie*
   Who would say the bird was lying

8 *never so*
   Like never before

Bottom

What do you see? You see an ass head of your own, [1] do
you?   [**Snout** exits.]

Enter **Quince**.

Quince

transformed   Bless thee, Bottom; bless thee. Thou art translated.°   105

He exits.

Bottom

I see their knavery: this is to make an ass of me, to
fright me if they could. But I will not stir from this
place, do what they can. I will walk up and down here,

so that   and I will sing, that° they shall hear I am not afraid.

blackbird   [*sings*] The ouzel° cock, so black of hue   110
With orange-tawny bill,

thrush   The throstle° with his note so true,
The wren with little quill[2]—

Titania

[*waking*] What angel wakes me from my flow'ry bed?

Bottom

[*sings*] The finch, the sparrow, and the lark,   115
The plainsong[3] cuckoo gray,
Whose note full many a man doth mark[4]
And dares not answer "Nay"[5]—

For indeed, who would set his wit to[6] so foolish a bird?
Who would give a bird the lie,[7] though he cry "cuckoo"   120
never so?[8]

Titania

I pray thee, gentle mortal, sing again.
Mine ear is much enamored of thy note;
So is mine eye enthrallèd to thy shape,

1   *thy fair virtue's force*

     The power of your fine qualities

2   *gleek upon occasion*

     Joke from time to time

3   *tend upon my state*

     Serve my exalted position

4   *purge thy mortal grossness*

     **I.e., separate your spirit from your
     physical being**

5   *Mote*

     **Both Quarto and Folio spell the
     fairy's name "Moth," which could
     indicate either the flying insect or a
     particle of dust (as at 5.1.305). As
     Shakespeare elsewhere only uses
     "moth" with negative connotations,
     it seems most likely that he
     intends the fairy's name to be the
     modern *Mote* (as here and in most
     recent editions).**

of necessity   And thy fair virtue's force[1] perforce° doth move me   125
On the first view to say, to swear, I love thee.
Bottom
Methinks, mistress, you should have little reason for
that, and yet, to say the truth, reason and love keep
little company together nowadays. The more the pity
that some honest neighbors will not make them   130
friends. Nay, I can gleek upon occasion.[2]
Titania
Thou art as wise as thou art beautiful.
Bottom
Not so, neither. But if I had wit enough to get out of
needs   this wood, I have enough to serve mine own turn.°
Titania
Out of this wood do not desire to go;   135
wish to   Thou shalt remain here whether thou wilt° or no.
value   I am a spirit of no common rate.°
always   The summer still° doth tend upon my state,[3]
And I do love thee. Therefore go with me.
I'll give thee fairies to attend on thee,   140
And they shall fetch thee jewels from the deep,
And sing while thou on pressèd flowers dost sleep;
And I will purge thy mortal grossness[4] so
That thou shalt like an airy spirit go.
—Peaseblossom, Cobweb, Mote,[5] and Mustardseed!   145

Enter four fairies [**Peaseblossom**, **Cobweb**, **Mote**,
and **Mustardseed**].

Peaseblossom
Ready.
Cobweb
            And I.

1 *crop their waxen thighs*

Gather the wax from their thighs

2 *I cry your worships' mercy*

I.e., I beg your pardon

Mote

     And I.

Mustardseed

      And I.

All

Where shall we go?

Titania

Be kind and courteous to this gentleman.

dance Hop in his walks and gambol° in his eyes.

apricots / blackberries Feed him with apricocks° and dewberries,°   150

With purple grapes, green figs, and mulberries.

bumblebees The honey bags steal from the humble-bees,°

candles And for night tapers° crop their waxen thighs[1]

And light them at the fiery glowworms' eyes

take To have° my love to bed and to arise;   155

And pluck the wings from painted butterflies

To fan the moonbeams from his sleeping eyes.

Nod to him, elves, and do him courtesies.

Peaseblossom

Hail, mortal.

Cobweb

    Hail.

Mote

     Hail.

Mustardseed

      Hail.

Bottom

I cry your worships' mercy,[2] heartily.—I beseech your 160
worship's name.

Cobweb

Cobweb.

1   *I shall desire you of more acquaitance*

    I look forward to knowing you
    better

2   *cut my finger*

    Cobwebs were used to stop
    bleeding.

3   *I know your patience well*

    I know well what trials you have
    had to endure

4   *ox-beef*

    Beef was often served with mustard;
    Bottom jokes that many of
    Mustardseed's relatives must have
    been turned into mustard and eaten
    with beef.

5   *enforcèd chastity*

    Antithetical meanings: it could
    refer either to forceful violation of
    chastity (i.e., rape), or to
    compelled chastity, one of the
    options Theseus offers Hermia in
    the form of life in a convent
    (1.1.70–73).

Bottom

I shall desire you of more acquaintance, [1] good Master
Cobweb. If I cut my finger, [2] I shall make bold with
you.—Your name, honest gentleman?   165

Peaseblossom

Peaseblossom.

Bottom

an unripe peapod   I pray you, commend me to Mistress Squash,° your
a ripe peapod   mother, and to Master Peascod,° your father. Good
Master Peaseblossom, I shall desire you of more
acquaintance too.— Your name, I beseech you, sir?   170

Mustardseed

Mustardseed.

Bottom

Good Master Mustardseed, I know your patience well. [3]
That same cowardly, giantlike ox-beef [4] hath devoured
many a gentleman of your house. I promise you your
kindred hath made my eyes water ere now. I desire you   175
of more acquaintance, good Master Mustardseed.

Titania

[*to the fairies*] Come; wait upon him. Lead him to my
    bower.
The moon methinks looks with a wat'ry eye,
And when she weeps, weeps every little flower,
Lamenting some enforcèd chastity. [5]   180
Tie up my love's tongue; bring him silently.

                                        [*They all*] *exit.*

1   *night-rule*

Night revels (with the sense also of
"disorder"). Night was often
considered a mysterious time
when the natural order was
subverted.

2   *rude mechanicals*

Unsophisticated workers. In
Shakespeare's England, *rude* had
stronger and more precise
connotations than simply
"impolite." As a designation of
social status, *rude*, in the sense of
"raw" or "rough," referred to the
unlearned, unrefined, or
uncivilized (*OED*). *Mechanicals* were
people who worked with their
hands, thus vulgar, coarse, and of
low social status (*OED*). The
attendant of a king, Robin feels
contempt for the artisans from his
sense of both his intellectual and
social superiority.

3   *stalls*

Storefronts or booths where a
tradesman could sell his goods

4   *shallowest thick-skin*

Stupidest brute

5   *russet-pated choughs, many in sort*

I.e., grey-headed jackdaws (crow-
like birds), gathered in a flock. The
term *russet* could describe a range
of colors from reddish-brown to
dark grey.

6   *his sight*

The sight of him

7   *at our stamp*

Robin is probably suggesting that he
frightened the mechanicals by
stamping his foot. Folktales from
Shakespeare's time often describe
how Robin activated his mischievous
spells by stamping his foot, though it
is possible what is meant is that
Robin and the ass-headed Bottom
make noises like hooved creatures
running.

Act 3, Scene 2

*Enter [**Oberon**,] King of Fairies.*

Oberon

I wonder if Titania be awaked,
Then what it was that next came in her eye,
Which she must dote on in extremity.

*Enter **Robin** Goodfellow.*

Here comes my messenger.—How now, mad spirit?
What night-rule¹ now about this haunted grove?   5

Robin

My mistress with a monster is in love.

secluded / holy   Near to her close° and consecrated° bower,

senseless   While she was in her dull° and sleeping hour,

fools   A crew of patches,° rude mechanicals²

That work for bread upon Athenian stalls,³   10

Were met together to rehearse a play
Intended for great Theseus' nuptial day.

brainless   The shallowest thick-skin⁴ of that barren° sort,

acted / play   Who Pyramus presented° in their sport,°

Abandoned / thicket   Forsook° his scene and entered in a brake,°   15

When I did him at this advantage take:

head   An ass's nole° I fixèd on his head.

Anon his Thisbe must be answerèd,

actor (i.e., Bottom)   And forth my mimic° comes. When they him spy,

bird hunter   As wild geese that the creeping fowler° eye,   20

Or russet-pated choughs, many in sort,⁵

loud noise   Rising and cawing at the gun's report,°

Scatter   Sever° themselves and madly sweep the sky—

So at his sight⁶ away his fellows fly;

And, at our stamp,⁷ here o'er and o'er one falls.   25

1   *help from Athens calls*

   Calls for help from Athens

2   *Their sense thus weak, lost with their*
   fears thus strong

   Their reason was in this way
   weakened, undermined by their
   strong fears

3   *Made senseless things begin to do*
   them wrong

   Began to believe that inanimate
   objects were trying to harm them

4   *From yielders all things catch.*

   I.e., everything seems to attack the
   fearful beings.

5   *Lay breath so bitter on your bitter foe.*

   Keep such bitter words for an
   enemy.

6   *but chide*

   Only scold

7   *o'er shoes*

   I.e., ankle-deep

He "Murder!" cries and help from Athens calls. [1]
Their sense thus weak, lost with their fears thus strong, [2]
Made senseless things begin to do them wrong, [3]
For briers and thorns at their apparel snatch—
Some sleeves, some hats. From yielders all things catch. [4]   30
I led them on in this distracted fear

transformed And left sweet Pyramus translated° there;
When in that moment, so it came to pass,
Titania waked and straightway loved an ass.

Oberon

This falls out better than I could devise.   35

ensnared But hast thou yet latched° the Athenian's eyes
With the love juice, as I did bid thee do?

Robin

I took him sleeping—that is finished too—
And the Athenian woman by his side,

necessity That, when he waked, of force° she must be eyed.   40

Enter **Demetrius** *and* **Hermia**.

Oberon

hidden [*to* **Robin**] Stand close.° This is the same Athenian.

                                                 [*They move aside.*]

Robin

[*aside*] This is the woman, but not this the man.

Demetrius

Oh, why rebuke you him that loves you so?
Lay breath so bitter on your bitter foe. [5]

Hermia

Now I but chide, [6] but I should use thee worse,   45
For thou, I fear, hast given me cause to curse.
If thou hast slain Lysander in his sleep,
Being o'er shoes [7] in blood, plunge in the deep

1   *displease / Her brother's noontide with*
    th' Antipodes

    I.e., "Disturb the sun's noonday light
    on the other side of the world." In
    Roman mythology, the sun god
    Apollo and the moon goddess Diana
    were siblings (hence *Her brother's*).

2   *Venus in her glimmering sphere*

    In Ptolemaic astronomy, the
    moon, sun, and planets were set in
    crystal spheres that orbited around
    the Earth (see 2.1.7 and note). *Venus*
    is of course the planet but also the
    Roman goddess of love, whose
    influence can be felt over the play
    (see line 107).

3   *What's this to*

    What does this have to do with

4   *Durst thou have looked upon him being*
    awake

    Would you have dared to look at
    him when he was awake

5   *for with doubler tongue / Than thine,*
    thou serpent, never adder stung

    I.e., because no *adder* (a poisonous
    snake) ever poisoned anyone with
    a more deceitful or forked *tongue*
    than yours.

6   *You spend your passion on a misprised*
    mood.

    You waste your energy with
    unjustified anger.

And kill me too.

The sun was not so true unto the day   50

As he to me. Would he have stolen away

readily   From sleeping Hermia? I'll believe as soon°

solid / drilled through   This whole° Earth may be bored,° and that the moon

May through the center creep and so displease

Her brother's noontide with th' Antipodes.[1]   55

It cannot be but thou hast murdered him:

deadly   So should a murderer look, so dead,° so grim.

Demetrius

So should the murdered look, and so should I,

Pierced through the heart with your stern cruelty.

Yet you, the murderer, look as bright, as clear,   60

As yonder Venus in her glimmering sphere.[2]

Hermia

What's this to[3] my Lysander? Where is he?

i.e., to me   Ah, good Demetrius, wilt thou give him me?°

Demetrius

I had rather give his carcass to my hounds.

Hermia

Out, dog! Out, cur! Thou driv'st me past the bounds   65

Of maiden's patience. Hast thou slain him then?

counted   Henceforth be never numbered° among men!

just once   Oh, once° tell true; tell true even for my sake.

Durst thou have looked upon him being awake,[4]

And hast thou killed him sleeping? O brave touch!   70

snake   Could not a worm,° an adder, do so much?

An adder did it, for with doubler tongue

Than thine, thou serpent, never adder stung.[5]

Demetrius

You spend your passion on a misprised mood.[6]

I am not guilty of Lysander's blood.   75

Nor is he dead, for aught that I can tell.

1   *So sorrow's heaviness doth heavier grow /*
    For debt that bankrupt sleep doth
    sorrow owe

    **The weight of sadness increases
    with the loss of sleep that
    accompanies it (*heaviness* could
    mean both "weight" and
    "sadness")**

2   *If for his tender here I make some stay*

    **If I stop and rest here, so that sleep
    can pay its debt**

3   *Then fate o'errules, that, one man hold-*
    ing troth, / A million fail, confounding
    oath on oath.

    **Then *fate* has taken over, since, for
    each man who keeps his word, a
    million fail to do so, breaking one
    vow after another.**

4   *look thou find*

    Be sure you find

5   *that costs the fresh blood dear*

    **Elizabethans believed that sighing
    consumed a person's blood,
    weakening the body.**

Hermia

I pray thee tell me then that he is well.

Demetrius

for that And if I could, what should I get therefor?°

Hermia

A privilege never to see me more,

And from thy hated presence part I so.   80

See me no more, whether he be dead or no.   *She exits.*

Demetrius

mood There is no following her in this fierce vein.°

Here therefore for awhile I will remain.

So sorrow's heaviness doth heavier grow

For debt that bankrupt sleep doth sorrow owe, [1]   85

Which now in some slight measure it will pay,

If for his tender here I make some stay. [2]

lies down [and sleeps]

Oberon

[*coming forward with* **Robin**] What hast thou done? Thou
    hast mistaken quite

And laid the love juice on some true love's sight.

mistake Of thy misprision° must perforce ensue   90

Some true love turned, and not a false turned true.

Robin

Then fate o'errules, that, one man holding troth,

A million fail, confounding oath on oath. [3]

Oberon

About the wood go swifter than the wind,

And Helena of Athens look thou find. [4]   95

lovesick / complexion All fancy-sick° she is and pale of cheer,°

With sighs of love that costs the fresh blood dear. [5]

By some illusion see thou bring her here.

in preparation for when I'll charm his eyes against° she do appear.

1 *Tartar's bow*

The Tartars, whose archery skills and superior bows were admired by the English, were a people of central Asia who at various times invaded other parts of Asia and eastern Europe.

2 *fond pageant*

Foolish spectacle

3 *sport alone*

Unsurpassed entertainment (or possibly merely "entertainment on its own")

4 *prepost'rously*

Etymologically, *preposterous* derives from *prae* (in front or before) and *posterus* (after or behind): hence "back first," or what we might colloquially call "ass backward." A concept often used in the Renaissance to describe inversions of social, gender, and sexual order, *preposterous* strongly connoted something monstrous, perverse, or contrary to the order of nature (*OED*). Robin's use of the word suggests the magnitude of the disorder in the forest that will need to be rectified before the young lovers and Bottom can reenter Athenian society.

Robin

I go; I go. Look how I go,   100
Swifter than arrow from the Tartar's bow. [1]   *[He exits.]*

Oberon

Flower of this purple dye,
Hit with Cupid's archery,
the pupil   Sink in apple° of his eye.

[squeezes flower into **Demetrius**'s eye]

spy   When his love he doth espy,°   105
Let her shine as gloriously
As the Venus of the sky.
When thou wak'st, if she be by,
relief (from lovesickness)   Beg of her for remedy.°

Enter [**Robin**].

Robin

Captain of our fairy band,   110
Helena is here at hand,
And the youth, mistook by me,
reward   Pleading for a lover's fee.°
Shall we their fond pageant [2] see?
Lord, what fools these mortals be!   115

Oberon

Stand aside. The noise they make
Will cause Demetrius to awake.

Robin

Then will two at once woo one.
That must needs be sport alone. [3]
And those things do best please me   120
That befall prepost'rously. [4]

*[***Robin** *and* **Oberon** *move aside.]*

1   *badge of faith*

    Mark of honesty (i.e., Lysander's tears)

2   *When truth kills truth, O devilish holy fray!*

    I.e., when the *truth* of one vow (to Helena) is used to wipe out the *truth* of another (to Hermia), the competition between them is both *devilish* (since one vow is broken) and *holy* (since devotion is pledged).

3   *give her o'er*

    Abandon her

4   *Weigh oath with oath, and you will nothing weigh.*

    Weigh your oath to Hermia against your oath to me, and (1) the scales will be evenly balanced; (2) both scales will be empty; (3) you, Lysander, will be found worthless (as an oath breaker).

5   *as light as tales*

    I.e., as worthless as lies

6   *ripe in show*

    Ripe looking

7   *high Taurus' snow*

    The snow of Taurus, a Turkish mountain range

8   *turns to a crow / When thou hold'st up thy hand*

    Looks as black as a crow compared to your white hand. Helena presumably holds up her hand protesting Demetrius's speech.

Enter **Lysander** *and* **Helena**.

Lysander

Why should you think that I should woo in scorn?

Scorn and derision never come in tears.

Look when I vow, I weep; and vows so born,

birth   In their nativity° all truth appears.   125

How can these things in me seem scorn to you,

Bearing the badge of faith [1] to prove them true?

Helena

You do advance your cunning more and more.

When truth kills truth, O devilish holy fray! [2]

are rightfully   These vows are° Hermia's. Will you give her o'er? [3]   130

Weigh oath with oath, and you will nothing weigh. [4]

Your vows to her and me, put in two scales,

Will even weigh, and both as light as tales. [5]

Lysander

I had no judgment when to her I swore.

Helena

Nor none, in my mind, now you give her o'er.   135

Lysander

Demetrius loves her, and he loves not you.

Demetrius

[*waking*] O Helen, goddess, nymph, perfect, divine!

eyes   To what, my love, shall I compare thine eyne?°

Crystal is muddy. Oh, how ripe in show [6]

Thy lips, those kissing cherries, tempting grow!   140

That pure congealèd white, high Taurus' snow, [7]

Fanned with the eastern wind, turns to a crow

When thou hold'st up thy hand. [8] Oh, let me kiss

promise   This princess of pure white, this seal° of bliss!

1 *set against*

   Attack; torment

2 *join in souls*

   Bond together; unite

3 *I will none.*

   I.e., I want nothing to do with her.

4 *My heart to her but as guest-wise*
   sojourned

   I.e., my heart merely visited her as a temporary guest; it was just a passing fancy.

Helena

O spite! O Hell! I see you all are bent   145
To set against[1] me for your merriment.
If you were civil and knew courtesy,
You would not do me thus much injury.
Can you not hate me, as I know you do,
But you must join in souls[2] to mock me too?   150

appearance If you were men, as men you are in show,°
You would not use a gentle lady so:

qualities To vow, and swear, and superpraise my parts,°
When I am sure you hate me with your hearts.
You both are rivals, and love Hermia,   155
And now both rivals to mock Helena—

fine A trim° exploit, a manly enterprise,
To conjure tears up in a poor maid's eyes
With your derision. None of noble sort

abuse Would so offend a virgin and extort°   160
A poor soul's patience, all to make you sport.

Lysander

You are unkind, Demetrius. Be not so,
For you love Hermia; this you know I know.
And here, with all good will, with all my heart,
In Hermia's love I yield you up my part;   165
And yours of Helena to me bequeath,
Whom I do love and will do till my death.

Helena

Never did mockers waste more idle breath.

Demetrius

Lysander, keep thy Hermia. I will none.[3]
If e'er I loved her, all that love is gone.   170
My heart to her but as guest-wise sojourned,[4]
And now to Helen is it home returned,
There to remain.

1   *aby it dear*

   Pay dearly for it

2   *The ear more quick of apprehension*
   makes

   Makes the ear more sensitive

3   *oes and eyes*

   I.e., stars. *Oes* were round sequins
   used in dressmaking; Lysander
   also puns on the *oh*'s and *I*'s of
   lovers' complaints.

4   *in spite of me*

   To spite me

Lysander

Helen, it is not so.

Demetrius

Disparage not the faith thou dost not know,
Lest to thy peril thou aby it dear. [1]   175
Look where thy love comes; yonder is thy dear.

Enter **Hermia**.

Hermia

its   Dark night, that from the eye his° function takes,
The ear more quick of apprehension makes. [2]
Insofar as   Wherein° it doth impair the seeing sense,
It pays the hearing double recompense.   180
Thou art not by mine eye, Lysander, found.
Mine ear, I thank it, brought me to thy sound.
But why unkindly didst thou leave me so?

Lysander

compel   Why should he stay whom love doth press° to go?

Hermia

What love could press Lysander from my side?   185

Lysander

stay   Lysander's love, that would not let him bide:°
gilds; decorates   Fair Helena, who more engilds° the night
Than all yon fiery oes and eyes [3] of light.
Why seek'st thou me? Could not this make thee know
The hate I bear thee made me leave thee so?   190

Hermia

You speak not as you think. It cannot be.

Helena

conspiracy   Lo, she is one of this confederacy!°
Now I perceive they have conjoined all three
To fashion this false sport in spite of me. [4]

1 *chid the hasty-footed time*

   Scolded swiftly passing time

2 *Two of the first, like coats in heraldry, / Due but to one and crownèd with one crest*

   Two of the same color, as in a coat-of-arms divided in half but granted to one person and with a single heraldic design. Helena again here suggests that she and Hermia are two parts of a single being, or *two seeming bodies but one heart* **(line 212).**

3 *Our sex*

   I.e., women in general

4 *Injurious Hermia! Most ungrateful maid! . . . / Our sex, as well as I, may chide you for it, / Though I alone do feel the injury.*

   Expressions of same-sex affection can be found throughout Shakespeare's sonnets and plays, including *The Merchant of Venice, As You Like It, Twelfth Night, Coriolanus,* **and** *The Two Noble Kinsmen.* **However, the Renaissance did not have the modern concepts of sexual identity and sexual orientation that we have inherited from 19th- and early 20th-century theories of human sexuality and psychology. Hence nobody in this period would have conceived of themselves in terms of modern sexual categories such as heterosexual and homosexual, or gay and straight. The challenge in reading passages such as this is to understand the personal, social, and political significance of same-sex relationships in Renaissance culture without applying anachronistic labels or standards of judgment. In Renaissance England, intimate relationships between women were generally accepted as long as they did not interfere with the women's conventional sexual and social duties: getting married, having children, maintaining chastity, and behaving in an appropriately feminine manner.** *In A Midsummer Night's Dream* **and** *As You Like It,* **adolescent female friendships finally give way to the new bonds between husbands and wives that signal entry into adulthood. However, being married did not prevent adult women from maintaining or establishing affectionate intimacies with other women through relationships of friendship, patronage, or service.**

5 *but now*

   Just recently

—Injurious Hermia! Most ungrateful maid!   195
Have you conspired, have you with these contrived,

torment To bait° me with this foul derision?

conversation Is all the counsel° that we two have shared,
The sisters' vows, the hours that we have spent
When we have chid the hasty-footed time [1]   200
For parting us? Oh, is all forgot?
All schooldays' friendship, childhood innocence?

artistically skilled We, Hermia, like two artificial° gods,
Have with our needles created both one flower,

piece of embroidery Both on one sampler,° sitting on one cushion,   205
Both warbling of one song, both in one key,
As if our hands, our sides, voices, and minds

united Had been incorporate.° So we grew together,
Like to a double cherry—seeming parted
But yet an union in partition—   210
Two lovely berries molded on one stem;
So, with two seeming bodies but one heart,
Two of the first, like coats in heraldry,
Due but to one and crownèd with one crest. [2]

tear And will you rend° our ancient love asunder   215
To join with men in scorning your poor friend?
It is not friendly; 'tis not maidenly.
Our sex, [3] as well as I, may chide you for it,
Though I alone do feel the injury. [4]

Hermia

I am amazèd at your words.   220
I scorn you not. It seems that you scorn me.

Helena

Have you not set Lysander, as in scorn,
To follow me and praise my eyes and face,
And made your other love, Demetrius—
Who even but now [5] did spurn me with his foot—   225

1 *setting on*

Urging

2 *What though*

So what if

3 *But miserable most, to love unloved*

But am the most miserable, to love and not be loved in return

4 *Counterfeit sad looks*

Pretend to be concerned

5 *Make mouths upon me*

Mock me

6 *This sport, well carried, shall be chronicled.*

This mockery, played successfully, will go down in history.

7 *You would not make me such an argument*

You would not make me such an object (of scorn)

8 *If she cannot entreat, I can compel.*

I.e., if her pleading cannot make you stop, I can force you to do so.

To call me goddess, nymph, divine, and rare,

Why Precious, celestial? Wherefore° speaks he this

To her he hates? And wherefore doth Lysander

Deny your love, so rich within his soul,

offer And tender° me, forsooth, affection,   230

But by your setting on,[1] by your consent?

favor What though[2] I be not so in grace° as you—

So hung upon with love, so fortunate—

But miserable most, to love unloved?[3]

This you should pity rather than despise.   235

Hermia

I understand not what you mean by this.

Helena

Persevere; keep it up Ay, do. Persever.° Counterfeit sad looks,[4]

Make mouths upon me[5] when I turn my back,

Wink each at other, hold the sweet jest up.

This sport, well carried, shall be chronicled.[6]   240

If you have any pity, grace, or manners,

You would not make me such an argument.[7]

But fare ye well. 'Tis partly my own fault,

Which death or absence soon shall remedy.

Lysander

Stay, gentle Helena. Hear my excuse.   245

My love, my life, my soul, fair Helena!

Helena

Oh, excellent!

Hermia

　　　　　　[*to* **Lysander**] Sweet, do not scorn her so.

Demetrius

If she cannot entreat, I can compel.[8]

Lysander

Thou canst compel no more than she entreat.

1   *that which I will lose for thee*

     I.e., my life

2   *Ethiope*

     **Ethiopian (referring to Hermia's
     dark hair and complexion,
     generally considered in
     Elizabethan England to be less
     attractive than fair features and
     probably the coloring of the boy
     actor who originally played the
     role)**

3   *Take on as you would follow*

     Act as if you are going to follow.

4   *tawny Tartar*

     Dark-skinned Turk

Thy threats have no more strength than her weak
   prayers.   250
—Helen, I love thee. By my life, I do.
I swear by that which I will lose for thee [1]
To prove him false that says I love thee not.

Demetrius

[*to* **Helena**] I say I love thee more than he can do.

Lysander

let's go off (and fight)   If thou say so, withdraw° and prove it too.   255

Demetrius

Quick, come.

Hermia

                      Lysander, whereto tends all this?

                                [*holds* **Lysander** *back*]

Lysander

[*to* **Hermia**] Away, you Ethiope! [2]

Demetrius

                      [*to* **Hermia**] No, no. He'll
Seem to break loose, [*to* **Lysander**] Take on as you
   would follow, [3]
cowardly   But yet come not. You are a tame° man; go!

Lysander

[*to* **Hermia**] Hang off, thou cat, thou burr! Vile thing,
   let loose,   260
Or I will shake thee from me like a serpent.

Hermia

Why are you grown so rude? What change is this,
Sweet love?

Lysander

                Thy "love"? Out, tawny Tartar, [4] out!
i.e., poison   Out, loathed med'cine!° O hated potion, hence!

Hermia

Do you not jest?

1   *I would I had your bond, for I perceive / A*
    weak bond holds you.

    **I wish you had signed a legal
    contract (*bond*) with me, because I
    see you don't keep your promises
    (but punning on the *weak bond*, or
    physical hold, Hermia currently
    has on Lysander).**

2   *What news*

    I.e., what do you mean?

3   *canker-blossom*

    Flower-eating grub

Helena

truly   Yes, sooth,° and so do you.   265

Lysander

(to duel)   Demetrius, I will keep my word° with thee.

Demetrius

I would I had your bond, for I perceive

A weak bond holds you. [1] I'll not trust your word.

Lysander

What? Should I hurt her, strike her, kill her dead?

Although I hate her, I'll not harm her so.   270

Hermia

[*to* **Lysander**] What? Can you do me greater harm than
    hate?

Why   Hate me? Wherefore?° O me! What news, [2] my love?

Am not I Hermia? Are not you Lysander?

before   I am as fair now as I was erewhile.°

Since night you loved me, yet since night you left me.   275

Why then, you left me—Oh, the gods forbid!—

In earnest, shall I say?

Lysander

                                   Ay, by my life,

And never did desire to see thee more.

Therefore be out of hope, of question, of doubt.

Be certain, nothing truer. 'Tis no jest   280

That I do hate thee and love Helena.

Hermia

deceiver   O me! [*to* **Helena**] You juggler!° You canker-blossom! [3]

You thief of love! What? Have you come by night

And stol'n my love's heart from him?

Helena

                                             Fine, i' faith!

Have you no modesty, no maiden shame,   285

1   *urged her height*

I.e., presented her height (to Lysander) as evidence of her worth

2   *painted maypole*

Maypoles were tall poles, decorated with ribbons, which were danced around during May Day festivities. By calling her *painted*, Hermia may also imply that Helena's beauty is the result of cosmetics.

3   *I was never curst. / I have no gift at all in shrewishness.*

Helena's description of Hermia as *curst* and *shrewish* might have reminded Shakespeare's audience of Katherine, the "shrew" in his earlier comedy *The Taming of the Shrew*. A shrew was a woman who was considered excessively outspoken or aggressive, especially toward authority figures such as husbands and fathers. Helena fears that the shrewish Hermia will thrash her, just as in *The Taming of the Shrew* Katherine physically abuses her younger sister. By evoking the possibility of physical violence, Shakespeare pushes the escalating conflict between Hermia and Helena in the direction of farce. On stage, the spectacle of an aggressive woman might provide excellent material for physical comedy and social satire, but in Renaissance England actual women regarded as shrews or scolds could face horrific punishments. A scold could be placed on the cucking stool, a chair attached to a lever that was used to dunk the victim in a lake or river. Worse, she could be fitted with a scold's bridle, an iron harness strapped to the head, with a metal tongue-piece that prevented the victim from talking and inflicted painful lacerations.

4   *in love unto*

Because of my love for

5   *chid me hence*

Driven me away with his rebukes

No touch of bashfulness? What? Will you tear
Impatient answers from my gentle tongue?
Fie, fie! You counterfeit, you puppet, you!

Hermia

"Puppet"? Why so?—Ay, that way goes the game.

comparison   Now I perceive that she hath made compare°   290
Between our statures. She hath urged her height, [1]
And with her personage, her tall personage,
Her height, forsooth, she hath prevailed with him.
—And are you grown so high in his esteem
Because I am so dwarfish and so low?   295
How low am I, thou painted maypole?[2] Speak.
How low am I? I am not yet so low
But that my nails can reach unto thine eyes.

Helena

[*to* **Lysander** *and* **Demetrius**] I pray you, though you
    mock me, gentlemen,

ill-tempered   Let her not hurt me. I was never curst.°   300
I have no gift at all in shrewishness.[3]

proper   I am a right° maid for my cowardice.
Let her not strike me. You perhaps may think,

somewhat   Because she is something° lower than myself,
That I can match her.

Hermia

                "Lower"? Hark, again!   305

Helena

Good Hermia, do not be so bitter with me.

always   I evermore° did love you, Hermia,
Did ever keep your counsels, never wronged you—

Except   Save° that in love unto[4] Demetrius

stealing away   I told him of your stealth° unto this wood.   310
He followed you; for love I followed him.
But he hath chid me hence[5] and threatened me

1 *To Athens will I bear my folly back*

   **I.e., I will take my foolish affection
   back to Athens**

2 *hind'ring knotgrass*

   **Knotgrass is a weed believed to
   stunt growth; Lysander implies
   that Hermia was raised on a diet of
   knotgrass (another joke about her
   size).**

3 *You are too officious / In her behalf that
   scorns your services.*

   **You are too presumptuous, acting
   on behalf of one who has
   contempt for your help.**

To strike me, spurn me—nay, to kill me too.

And now, so you will let me quiet go,

To Athens will I bear my folly back [1]   315

And follow you no further. Let me go.

foolish   You see how simple and how fond° I am.

Hermia

Why, get you gone! Who is 't that hinders you?

Helena

A foolish heart that I leave here behind.

Hermia

What? With Lysander?

Helena

                  With Demetrius.   320

Lysander

Be not afraid. She shall not harm thee, Helena.

Demetrius

[*to* **Lysander**] No, sir, she shall not, though you take

    her part.

Helena

harsh / shrewish   Oh, when she's angry, she is keen° and shrewd!°

She was a vixen when she went to school,

And, though she be but little, she is fierce.   325

Hermia

"Little" again? Nothing but "low" and "little"!

insult   —Why will you suffer her to flout° me thus?

Let me come to her.

Lysander

               [*to* **Hermia**] Get you gone, you dwarf,

smallest thing (Latin)   You *minimus*° of hind'ring knotgrass [2] made,

You bead, you acorn!

Demetrius

              You are too officious   330

In her behalf that scorns your services. [3]

1   *Never so little show of love*

    **I.e., even a tiny demonstration of
    love**

2   *to try whose right, / Of thine or mine, is
    most in Helena*

    **To test which of us has the greatest
    claim to Helena**

3   *cheek by jowl*

    I.e., side by side

4   *shadows*

    **Spirits (but, *shadows* also means
    "darkness," as well as "illusions,"
    realms that Oberon also rules over)**

5   *so far*

    To this extent

Let her alone. Speak not of Helena.

Take not her part. For if thou dost intend

Never so little show of love[1] to her,

pay for   Thou shalt aby° it.

Lysander

                Now she holds me not.   335

Now follow, if thou dar'st, to try whose right,

Of thine or mine, is most in Helena.[2]

Demetrius

"Follow"? Nay, I'll go with thee, cheek by jowl.[3]

                [**Lysander** *and* **Demetrius** *exit.*]

Hermia

trouble / because   You, mistress, all this coil° is long° of you.

Nay, go not back.

Helena

                I will not trust you, I,   340

ill-tempered   Nor longer stay in your curst° company.

fight   Your hands than mine are quicker for a fray.°

My legs are longer, though, to run away.

Hermia

I am amazed and know not what to say.

             [**Hermia** *and* **Helena** *separately*] *exit.*

Oberon

Always   [*coming forward with* **Robin**] This is thy negligence. Still°

    thou mistak'st,   345

Or else committ'st thy knaveries willfully.

Robin

Believe me, King of shadows,[4] I mistook.

Did not you tell me I should know the man

By the Athenian garments he had on?

And so far[5] blameless proves my enterprise   350

That I have 'nointed an Athenian's eyes.

turn out   And so far am I glad it so did sort,°

1   *Acheron*

     In Greek mythology, Acheron was
     one of the four rivers of Hell.

2   *frame thy tongue*

     Fashion your voice

3   *With league whose date till death shall*
     never end

     I.e., in a bond of friendship that
     will last until death

4   *night's swift dragons*

     Dragons were often said to pull the
     chariot of night.

5   *Aurora's harbinger*

     I.e., the morning star. Aurora was
     the Greek goddess of the dawn.

arguing   As this their jangling° I esteem a sport.

Oberon

Thou see'st these lovers seek a place to fight.

Hurry   Hie° therefore, Robin, overcast the night.   355

sky   The starry welkin° cover thou anon

With drooping fog as black as Acheron,¹

And lead these testy rivals so astray

That   As° one come not within another's way.

Like to Lysander sometime frame thy tongue,²   360

Then stir Demetrius up with bitter wrong,

rant   And sometime rail° thou like Demetrius;

And from each other look thou lead them thus,

Till o'er their brows death-counterfeiting sleep

batlike   With leaden legs and batty° wings doth creep.   365

[*gives* **Robin** *a flower*]

Then crush this herb into Lysander's eye,

potent   Whose liquor hath this virtuous° property:

its   To take from thence all error with his° might

normal   And make his eyeballs roll with wonted° sight.

When they next wake, all this derision   370

Shall seem a dream and fruitless vision,

go   And back to Athens shall the lovers wend,°

duration   With league whose date° till death shall never end.³

Whiles I in this affair do thee employ,

I'll to my Queen and beg her Indian boy,   375

And then I will her charmèd eye release

From monster's view, and all things shall be peace.

Robin

My fairy lord, this must be done with haste,

For night's swift dragons⁴ cut the clouds full fast,

And yonder shines Aurora's harbinger,⁵   380

At whose approach, ghosts, wandering here and there,

Troop home to churchyards. Damnèd spirits all,

1   *crossways and floods*

People who committed suicide were denied burial in consecrated ground and were instead buried at crossroads. *Floods* refers either to the waters in which people have drowned themselves or in which they have accidentally drowned, but in either case those drowned were denied proper burial rites.

2   *But we are sprits of another sort.*

Oberon distinguishes between the relatively benevolent fairies of the play and the more sinister figures of ghosts. According to Catholic doctrine, ghosts were spirits of the dead that came from Purgatory to walk the earth. Since Protestant theologians rejected the existence of Purgatory and held that the spirits of the dead remained in Heaven or Hell, they proposed that ghosts usually were demonic agents that attempted to lead human beings into sin.

3   *the morning's love*

Oberon could be alluding to trysts he has had with the goddess Aurora, or mean that he has hunted with Aurora's would-be lover, Cepahlus (see 5.1.195 and note).

4   *the eastern gate*

I.e., the point of sunrise

That in crossways and floods[1] have burial,

Already to their wormy beds are gone.

For fear lest day should look their shames upon,   385

They willfully themselves exile from light

ever   And must for aye° consort with black-browed night.

Oberon

But we are spirits of another sort.[2]

I with the morning's love[3] have oft made sport,

gamekeeper   And like a forester° the groves may tread   390

Even till the eastern gate,[4] all fiery red,

i.e., the sea   Opening on Neptune° with fair blessèd beams,

Turns into yellow gold his salt green streams.

But notwithstanding, haste. Make no delay.

We may effect this business yet ere day.   [**Oberon** *exits.*]   395

Robin

Up and down, up and down,

I will lead them up and down.

I am feared in field and town.

Goblin, lead them up and down.

Here comes one.   400

Enter **Lysander**.

Lysander

Where art thou, proud Demetrius? Speak thou now.

Robin

With sword drawn   [*as* **Demetrius**] Here, villain. Drawn° and ready. Where

art thou?

Lysander

immediately   I will be with thee straight.°

Robin

[*as* **Demetrius**] Follow me then

1   *He is defiled / That draws a sword on*
    thee.

    **I.e., it would be shameful to
    confront you with a sword (since
    you are not a worthy opponent).**

2   *We'll try no manhood here.*

    **We will not test our manliness (by
    dueling) here.**

more level To plainer° ground. [**Lysander** *exits.*]

Enter **Demetrius**.

Demetrius

Lysander, speak again!

Thou runaway, thou coward, art thou fled?   405

Speak! In some bush? Where dost thou hide thy head?

Robin

[*as* **Lysander**] Thou coward, art thou bragging to the stars,

Telling the bushes that thou look'st for wars,

coward And wilt not come? Come, recreant.° Come, thou child!

I'll whip thee with a rod. He is defiled   410

That draws a sword on thee. ¹

Demetrius

Yea, art thou there?

Robin

[*as* **Lysander**] Follow my voice. We'll try no manhood

here. ²   *They exit.*

[*Enter* **Lysander**.]

Lysander

He goes before me and still dares me on.

When I come where he calls, then he is gone.

quicker The villain is much lighter-heeled° than I.   415

I followed fast, but faster he did fly,

That fallen am I in dark uneven way,

And here will rest me.   [*lies down*]

Come, thou gentle day,

For if but once thou show me thy gray light,

insult I'll find Demetrius and revenge this spite.°   [*sleeps*]   420

1   *buy this dear*

Pay dearly for this

2   *Faintness constraineth me / To measure*

out my length on this cold bed.

Exhaustion leads me to lay my
body down on this cold ground.

[Enter] **Robin** *and* **Demetrius**.

Robin

[*as* **Lysander** *to* **Demetrius**] Ho, ho, ho! Coward, why
     com'st thou not?

Demetrius

Wait for / know   Abide° me, if thou dar'st! For well I wot°
     Thou runn'st before me, shifting every place,
     And dar'st not stand nor look me in the face.
     Where art thou now?

Robin

                              [*as* **Lysander**] Come hither. I am here.   *425*

Demetrius

     Nay, then, thou mock'st me. Thou shalt buy this dear[1]
     If ever I thy face by daylight see.
     Now go thy way. Faintness constraineth me
     To measure out my length on this cold bed.[2]
     By day's approach look to be visited. [*lies down and sleeps*]   *430*

Enter **Helena**.

Helena

     O weary night, O long and tedious night,
Shorten   Abate° thy hours. Shine comforts from the east
     That I may back to Athens by daylight
     From these that my poor company detest,
     And sleep, that sometimes shuts up sorrow's eye,   *435*
     Steal me awhile from mine own company.
                              [*lies down and sleeps*]

Robin

     Yet but three? Come one more:
     Two of both kinds make up four.
ill-tempered   Here she comes, curst° and sad.

1   *a fray*

I.e., to fight

[*Enter* **Hermia**.]

mischievous   Cupid is a knavish° lad   440

Thus to make poor females mad.

Hermia

Never so weary, never so in woe,

Bedabbled with the dew and torn with briers,

I can no further crawl, no further go.

My legs can keep no pace with my desires.   445

Here will I rest me till the break of day.

Heavens shield Lysander if they mean a fray! [1]

                              [*lies down and sleeps*]

Robin

On the ground

Sleep sound.

I'll apply   450

To your eye,

Gentle lover, remedy.

                        [*squeezes flower into* **Lysander**'s *eyes*]

When thou wak'st,

Thou tak'st

True delight   455

In the sight

Of thy former lady's eye.

And the country proverb known,

That every man should take his own,

In your waking shall be shown.   460

Jack shall have Jill.

Nought shall go ill.

The man shall have his mare again, and all shall be well.

                                        [*He exits.*]

1   still sleep

The scene is continuous with the
previous one, though the act break
is marked in the Folio of 1623. In
performance there is no break, and
the lovers remain asleep on stage,
unnoticed until line 126.

Act 4, Scene 1

[**Lysander**, **Demetrius**, **Helena**, *and* **Hermia** *still sleep.*] [1]
Enter [**Titania**,] *Queen of* [*the*] *Fairies; and* [**Bottom**, *with the*
ass's head;] *and fairies* [**Peaseblossom**, **Cobweb**, **Mote**,
Mustardseed]; *and* [**Oberon**] *the King behind them*, [*unseen*].

Titania

[*to* **Bottom**] Come. Sit thee down upon this flow'ry bed

lovable / caress   While I thy amiable° cheeks do coy,°

And stick musk-roses in thy sleek, smooth head,

And kiss thy fair large ears, my gentle joy.

Bottom

Where's Peaseblossom?   5

Peaseblossom

Ready.

Bottom

Scratch my head, Peaseblossom.—Where's Monsieur
Cobweb?

Cobweb

Ready.

Bottom

Monsieur Cobweb, good monsieur, get you your weap-   10
ons in your hand and kill me a red-hipped humble-bee
on the top of a thistle. And, good monsieur, bring me
the honey bag. Do not fret yourself too much in the
action, monsieur. And good monsieur, have a care the

unwilling   honey bag break not: I would be loath° to have you   15

flooded   overflown° with a honey bag, signior.   [**Cobweb** *exits.*]
—Where's Monsieur Mustardseed?

Mustardseed

Ready.

1   *leave your courtesy*

    I.e., do not bow

2   *Cavaliery Cobweb*

    **Bottom means *Cavaliere*, an Italian
    form of respectful address to a
    gentleman. *Cobweb*, however, must
    be an error since *Cobweb* has been
    sent to get honey (lines 10–13), and
    it is Peaseblossom who has been
    asked to scratch Bottom's head
    (line 7).**

3   *the tongs and the bones*

    **Rustic musical instruments: *the
    tongs* were chimes similar to a
    triangle; *the bones* were bone
    clappers like castanets.**

4   *exposition of*

    I.e., "disposition to"

5   *be always away*

    **I.e., depart and stay away (to allow
    her to be alone with Bottom)**

Bottom

fist Give me your neaf,° Monsieur Mustardseed. Pray you,
leave your courtesy,¹ good monsieur. 20

Mustardseed

What's your will?

Bottom

Nothing, good monsieur, but to help Cavaliery Cobweb²
to scratch. I must to the barber's, monsieur, for

marvelously methinks I am marvelous° hairy about the face. And I
am such a tender ass, if my hair do but tickle me, I must 25
scratch.

Titania

What? Wilt thou hear some music, my sweet love?

Bottom

I have a reasonable good ear in music. Let's have the
tongs and the bones.³ [*Music plays.*]

Titania

Or say, sweet love, what thou desirest to eat. 30

Bottom

animal feed Truly, a peck of provender.° I could munch your good
bundle dry oats. Methinks I have a great desire to a bottle° of
equal hay. Good hay, sweet hay, hath no fellow.°

Titania

adventurous I have a venturous° fairy that shall seek
The squirrel's hoard and fetch thee new nuts. 35

Bottom

I had rather have a handful or two of dried peas. But, I
pray you, let none of your people stir me. I have an
exposition of⁴ sleep come upon me.

Titania

Sleep thou, and I will wind thee in my arms.
Fairies, be gone, and be always away.⁵ [**Fairies** *exit.*] 40

1   *woodbine*

    See 2.1.253 and note.

2   *of late*

    Recently

3   *favors*

    Love tokens; perhaps the garland
    of flowers Bottom now wears

4   *Like tears that did their own disgrace
    bewail*

    Like tears shed over their own
    disgrace (in being used to decorate
    an ass)

5   *fierce vexation*

    Powerful disturbance

So doth the woodbine[1] the sweet honeysuckle
Gently entwist. The female ivy so
Enrings the barky fingers of the elm.
Oh, how I love thee! How I dote on thee!

[**Titania** *and* **Bottom** *sleep.*]

Enter **Robin** *Goodfellow.*

Oberon

Welcome, good Robin. See'st thou this sweet sight?   45

infatuation   Her dotage° now I do begin to pity,

For meeting her of late[2] behind the wood,

Seeking sweet favors[3] for this hateful fool,

rebuke   I did upbraid° her and fall out with her,

For she his hairy temples then had rounded   50

crown   With coronet° of fresh and fragrant flowers,

And that same dew, which sometime on the buds

accustomed / lustrous   Was wont° to swell like round and orient° pearls,

small flowers   Stood now within the pretty flow'rets'° eyes

Like tears that did their own disgrace bewail.[4]   55

When I had at my pleasure taunted her,

And she in mild terms begged my patience,

I then did ask of her her changeling child,

Which straight she gave me and her fairy sent

To bear him to my bower in Fairyland.   60

And now I have the boy, I will undo

This hateful imperfection of her eyes.

And, gentle puck, take this transformèd scalp

laborer   From off the head of this Athenian swain,°

others   That, he awaking when the other° do,   65

return   May all to Athens back again repair°

And think no more of this night's accidents

But as the fierce vexation[5] of a dream.

1   *Dian's bud o'er Cupid's flower*

    Oberon associates the herb used as
    an antidote to the love potion with
    the chaste goddess Diana, while
    the original potion is associated
    with Cupid.

2   *these five*

    I.e., the two couples and Bottom,
    all asleep

But first I will release the Fairy Queen.

[*squeezing flower into* **Titania**'s *eyes*] Be as thou wast wont
   to be.   70

See as thou wast wont to see.

Dian's bud o'er Cupid's flower [1]

Hath such force and blessèd power.

Now, my Titania, wake you, my sweet Queen.

Titania

[*waking*] My Oberon, what visions have I seen!   75

Methought I was enamored of an ass.

Oberon

There lies your love.

Titania

               How came these things to pass?

face   Oh, how mine eyes do loathe his visage° now!

Oberon

Silence awhile.—Robin, take off this head.

—Titania, music call, and strike more dead   80

Than common sleep of all these five [2] the sense.

Titania

Music, ho! Music such as charmeth sleep!

                    [*Gentle music plays.*]

Robin

[*taking the ass's head off* **Bottom**] Now when thou wak'st,
   with thine own fool's eyes peep.

Oberon

Sound, music! [*Lively music plays.*]—Come, my Queen, take
   hands with me,

And rock the ground whereon these sleepers be.   85

                     [*They dance.*]

friendship   Now thou and I are new in amity,°

ceremoniously   And will tomorrow midnight solemnly°

Dance in Duke Theseus' house triumphantly,

1   *our observation*

     I.e., our performance of the May
     Day ceremonies

2   *since we have the vaward of the day*

     Since it is still early in the day

3   *the music of my hounds*

     Hunting dogs were valued in
     Elizabethan England as much for
     the *music* of their barking and
     howling as for their hunting ability.

4   *Uncouple*

     Unleash (hunting dogs were
     leashed in pairs)

5   *Of hounds and echo in conjunction*

     Of the barking of the hounds and
     its echo sounding together

And bless it to all fair prosperity.

There shall the pairs of faithful lovers be   90

joy   Wedded, with Theseus, all in jollity.°

Robin

Fairy King, attend and mark:

I do hear the morning lark.

Oberon

sober; serious   Then, my Queen, in silence sad,°

Trip we after the night's shade.   95

encircle   We the globe can compass° soon,

Swifter than the wand'ring moon.

Titania

Come, my lord, and in our flight,

Tell me how it came this night

That I sleeping here was found   100

With these mortals on the ground.

[**Oberon**, **Titania**, *and* **Robin**] *exit.*

Wind horn [*within.*]

Enter **Theseus** [*with* **Hippolyta** *and* **Egeus**,] *and all his train.*

Theseus

Go, one of you; find out the forester,

For now our observation [1] is performed,

vanguard   And, since we have the vaward° of the day, [2]

My love shall hear the music of my hounds. [3]   105

Uncouple [4] in the western valley. Let them go.

Dispatch, I say, and find the forester.   [*An attendant exits.*]

We will, fair Queen, up to the mountain's top

intermingling   And mark the musical confusion°

Of hounds and echo in conjunction. [5]   110

1   *Hercules and Cadmus*

     Hercules was a famous hero of
     classical myth; *Cadmus* was the
     legendary founder of the city of
     Thebes

2   *hounds of Sparta*

     Spartan hounds were famous for
     their hunting abilities.

3   *gallant chiding*

     Impressive barking

4   *flewed*

     With large, fleshy jowls

5   *dew-lapped*

     With drooping folds of skin
     hanging from the neck

6   *matched in mouth like bells, / Each
     under each*

     With voices harmoniously tuned
     like a set of bells

7   *holla'd*

     Holla being a traditional hunting
     cry

8   *in grace of our solemnity*

     I.e., in honor of our May Day
     festivities

Hippolyta

I was with Hercules and Cadmus[1] once,

cornered When in a wood of Crete they bayed° the bear

With hounds of Sparta.[2] Never did I hear

Such gallant chiding,[3] for, besides the groves,

The skies, the fountains, every region near 115

Seemed all one mutual cry. I never heard

So musical a discord, such sweet thunder.

Theseus

My hounds are bred out of the Spartan kind,

sand-colored So flewed,[4] so sanded,° and their heads are hung

With ears that sweep away the morning dew, 120

Crook-kneed and dew-lapped[5] like Thessalian bulls,

Slow in pursuit, but matched in mouth like bells,

melodious Each under each.[6] A cry more tunable°

Was never holla'd[7] to, nor cheered with horn,

In Crete, in Sparta, nor in Thessaly. 125

wait Judge when you hear. [*sees the sleeping lovers*] But, soft!°

What nymphs are these?

Egeus

My lord, this is my daughter here asleep.

And this, Lysander. This Demetrius is.

This Helena, old Nedar's Helena.

at I wonder of° their being here together. 130

Theseus

No doubt they rose up early to observe

The rite of May, and, hearing our intent,

Came here in grace of our solemnity.[8]

But speak, Egeus: is not this the day

That Hermia should give answer of her choice? 135

Egeus

It is, my lord.

1 *Saint Valentine is past. / Begin these woodbirds but to couple now?*

It was proverbially believed that birds chose their mates on Valentine's Day.

2 *sleep by hate*

I.e., sleep next to your hated enemy

Theseus

Go bid the huntsmen wake them with their horns.

[An attendant exits.]

Shout within. [**Lysander**, **Demetrius**, **Helena**,
and **Hermia** *wake and*] *start up. Wind horns.*

Good morrow, friends. Saint Valentine is past.

Begin these woodbirds but to couple now?[1]

[**Lysander**, **Demetrius**, **Helena**, *and* **Hermia** *kneel.*]

Lysander

Pardon, my lord.

Theseus

I pray you all, stand up.   140

[**Lysander**, **Demetrius**, **Helena**, *and* **Hermia** *stand.*]

[*to* **Lysander** *and* **Demetrius**] I know you two are rival
   enemies.

How comes this gentle concord in the world,

suspicion   That hatred is so far from jealousy°

To sleep by hate[2] and fear no enmity?

Lysander

with bewilderment   My lord, I shall reply amazèdly,°   145

Half sleep, half waking. But, as yet, I swear

I cannot truly say how I came here,

But as I think—for truly would I speak,

And now I do bethink me, so it is—

I came with Hermia hither. Our intent   150

Was to be gone from Athens, where we might,

Beyond   Without° the peril of the Athenian law—

Egeus

[*to* **Theseus**] Enough, enough, my lord. You have enough!

I beg the law, the law, upon his head.

—They would have stol'n away, they would, Demetrius,   155

Thereby to have defeated you and me:

You of your wife and me of my consent,

1　*idle gaud*

Worthless bauble

2　*something worn*

I.e., near its end

Of my consent that she should be your wife.

Demetrius

[*to* **Theseus**] My lord, fair Helen told me of their stealth,

Of this their purpose hither to this wood,   160

And I in fury hither followed them,

love   Fair Helena in fancy° following me.

know   But, my good lord, I wot° not by what power

(But by some power it is) my love to Hermia,

Melted as the snow, seems to me now   165

As the remembrance of an idle gaud [1]

Which in my childhood I did dote upon;

And all the faith, the virtue of my heart,

The object and the pleasure of mine eye,

Is only Helena. To her, my lord,   170

Was I betrothed ere I saw Hermia,

But like in sickness did I loathe this food,

i.e., having returned   But, as in health, come° to my natural taste,

Now I do wish it, love it, long for it,

And will for evermore be true to it.   175

Theseus

Fair lovers, you are fortunately met.

presently   Of this discourse we more will hear anon.°

overrule   —Egeus, I will overbear° your will,

For in the temple by and by with us

These couples shall eternally be knit.   180

since   —And, for° the morning now is something worn, [2]

intended   Our purposed° hunting shall be set aside.

Away with us to Athens. Three and three,

ceremony   We'll hold a feast in great solemnity.°

Come, Hippolyta.   185

[**Theseus**, **Hippolyta**, **Egeus**, *and train exit.*]

Demetrius

These things seem small and undistinguishable,

1   *Mine own, and not mine own*

Mine (because I found him), but
not mine (since he once belonged
to someone else)

2   *Heigh-ho!*

An exclamation, perhaps
accompanying a yawn, but also
with some residue of the "hee-
haw" of the ass

3   *God's my life*

God save my life (a mild oath)

Like far-off mountains turnèd into clouds.

Hermia

divided; unfocused Methinks I see these things with parted° eye,

When everything seems double.

Helena

So methinks,

And I have found Demetrius like a jewel, 190

Mine own, and not mine own. [1]

Demetrius

Are you sure

That we are awake? It seems to me

That yet we sleep, we dream. Do not you think

The Duke was here and bid us follow him?

Hermia

Yea, and my father.

Helena

And Hippolyta. 195

Lysander

And he did bid us follow to the temple.

Demetrius

Why then, we are awake. Let's follow him,

And by the way let us recount our dreams.

[**Lysander, Demetrius, Helena,** *and* **Hermia** *exit.*]

Bottom

[*waking*] When my cue comes, call me, and I will answer.

i.e., next cue My next° is "Most fair Pyramus." Heigh-ho! [2] Peter 200

Quince? Flute the bellows-mender? Snout the tinker?

Starveling? God's my life, [3] stol'n hence and left me

asleep? I have had a most rare vision. I have had a

dream past the wit of man to say what dream it was.

explain Man is but an ass if he go about to expound° this dream. 205

Methought I was—there is no man can tell what. Me-

thought I was, and methought I had—but man is but

1   *a patched fool*

Fools and jesters were known by
their colorful patchwork clothing.

2   *The eye of man hath not heard, the ear of*
man hath not seen, man's hand is not
able to taste, his tongue to conceive, nor
his heart to report what my dream was.

Bottom garbles a passage from
Paul's First Epistle to the
Corinthians (2: 9–10). Paul's
contrast between "the wisdom of
this world" and "the wisdom of
God" challenges the kind of
political authority represented by
Duke Theseus in the play: "And we
speak wisdom among them that
are perfect: not the wisdom of this
world, neither of the princes of this
world, which come to nought. But
we speak the wisdom of God in a
mystery, even the hidden wisdom,
which God determined before the
world, unto our glory. Which none
of the princes of this world hath
known: for had they known it, they
would not have crucified the Lord
of glory. But as it is written, the
things which eye hath not seen,
neither ear hath heard, neither
came into the heart of man, are
which God hath prepared for them
that love him. But God hath
revealed them unto us by his spirit:
for the spirit searcheth all things,
yea, the deep things of God" (1 Cor
2: 6–10, Geneva trans., 1560).

3   *it hath no bottom*

I.e., it cannot be fully understood
(but also "has no foundation in
reality")

a patched fool[1] if he will offer to say what methought I
had. The eye of man hath not heard, the ear of man
hath not seen, man's hand is not able to taste, his   210
tongue to conceive, nor his heart to report what my
dream was.[2] I will get Peter Quince to write a ballad of
this dream. It shall be called "Bottom's Dream" because it
hath no bottom.[3] And I will sing it in the latter end of a
play before the Duke. Peradventure,° to make it the   215
more gracious, I shall sing it at her° death.   [*He exits.*]

Perhaps — Peradventure,°
(i.e., Thisbe's) — her°

1   *paramour*

    Quince, as Flute points out, means to say *paragon* (model of excellence); a *paramour* is a lover.

2   *a thing of naught*

    A wicked thing

3   *we had all been made men*

    I.e., we would have made our fortunes

4   *sixpence a day*

    Flute suggests that Theseus would have been so impressed with Bottom's performance that he would have given him a pension of sixpence a day, a sizeable sum for a craftsman.

5   *He could not have 'scaped sixpence a day.*

    He couldn't have given any less than a pension of six pence a day.

Act 4, Scene 2

Enter **Quince**, **Flute**, [**Snout**, *and* **Starveling**].

Quince

Have you sent to Bottom's house? Is he come home
yet?

Starveling

carried off He cannot be heard of. Out of doubt he is transported.°

Flute

If he come not, then the play is marred. It goes not
forward. Doth it?   5

Quince

It is not possible. You have not a man in all Athens able
perform to discharge° Pyramus but he.

Flute

intellect / working No, he hath simply the best wit° of any handicraft° man
in Athens.

Quince

appearance Yea, and the best person° too, and he is a very paramour[1]   10
for a sweet voice.

Flute

You must say "paragon." A "paramour" is, God bless us,
a thing of naught.[2]

Enter **Snug** *the joiner.*

Snug

Masters, the Duke is coming from the temple, and there is
two or three lords and ladies more married. If our sport   15
had gone forward, we had all been made men.[3]

Flute

worthy O sweet bully° Bottom! Thus hath he lost sixpence a day[4]
during his life. He could not have 'scaped sixpence a day.[5]

1 *right as it fell out*

Exactly as it happened

2 *good strings to your beards*

Strong *strings* with which to tie on
your false beards

3 *preferred*

Chosen. In 5.1.42–81, however, it is
clear that their play has not yet
been selected but merely been
placed on the short list of plays to
be considered.

_If_   An° the Duke had not given him sixpence a day for playing Pyramus, I'll be hanged. He would have deserved it.   20
Sixpence a day in Pyramus, or nothing.

Enter **Bottom.**

Bottom

good fellows   Where are these lads? Where are these hearts?°

Quince

i.e., auspicious   Bottom! O most courageous° day! O most happy hour!

Bottom

speak of   Masters, I am to discourse° wonders—but ask me not
what, for if I tell you, I am no true Athenian. I will tell   25
you everything right as it fell out. [1]

Quince

Let us hear, sweet Bottom.

Bottom

Not a word of me. All that I will tell you is that the Duke
hath dined. Get your apparel together, good strings to

shoes   your beards, [2] new ribbons to your pumps.° Meet pres-   30
ently at the palace. Every man look o'er his part. For the
short and the long is, our play is preferred! [3] In any
case, let Thisbe have clean linen. And let not him that
plays the lion pare his nails, for they shall hang out for
the lion's claws, and, most dear actors, eat no onions   35
nor garlic, for we are to utter sweet breath, and I do not
doubt but to hear them say, "It is a sweet comedy." No
more words. Away, go away!   [_They exit._]

1   *antique fables*

Q1 has "antique" (ancient); Q2 and F
have "anticke" (antic, grotesque, or
theatrical). Theseus might be saying
that he does not believe old myths
about fairies, or that such stories are
too obviously artificial to take
seriously.

2   *shaping fantasies*

Active imaginations

3   *all compact*

Entirely composed

4   *all as frantic*

Equally frenzied

5   *Helen's beauty*

Helen of Troy was proverbially the
most beautiful woman who ever
lived.

6   *brow of Egypt*

I.e., the dark complexion of a gypsy
(gypsies were thought to have
come from Egypt, hence their
name)

7   *bodies forth*

Makes tangible

8   *gives to airy nothing / A local habitation
and a name*

I.e., takes imagined things and
gives them a recognizable form
and a name

9   *It comprehends some bringer of that joy*

It introduces in a source of the joy

10   *transfigured so together*

Affected in the same manner

Act 5, Scene 1

Enter **Theseus**, **Hippolyta**, *and* **Philostrate**, [*with other lords and attendants*].

Hippolyta

what   'Tis strange, my Theseus, that° these lovers speak of.

Theseus

More strange than true. I never may believe

tales   These antique fables [1] nor these fairy toys.°

boiling; frenetic   Lovers and madmen have such seething° brains,

intuit; imagine   Such shaping fantasies, [2] that apprehend°   5

understands   More than cool reason ever comprehends.°

The lunatic, the lover, and the poet

Are of imagination all compact. [3]

One sees more devils than vast Hell can hold:

That is the madman. The lover, all as frantic, [4]   10

Sees Helen's beauty [5] in a brow of Egypt. [6]

The poet's eye, in a fine frenzy rolling,

Doth glance from Heaven to Earth, from Earth to
    Heaven,

And, as imagination bodies forth [7]

The forms of things unknown, the poet's pen   15

Turns them to shapes and gives to airy nothing

A local habitation and a name. [8]

Such tricks hath strong imagination,

That if it would but apprehend some joy

It comprehends some bringer of that joy; [9]   20

Or in the night, imagining some fear,

thought to be   How easy is a bush supposed° a bear!

Hippolyta

But all the story of the night told over,

And all their minds transfigured so together, [10]

1   *More witnesseth than fancy's images /*
And grows to something of great con-
stancy, / But, howsoever, strange and
admirable

I.e., signifies more than mere delusion and grows into something consistent and believable, though admittedly unusual and wondrous

2   **Philostrate**

The Quarto and Folio assign the following speeches to different characters. In Q (and here), Theseus reads the list of entertainments, and Philostrate, the courtier who briefly appears in the first scene of the play, discourages him from choosing "Pyramus and Thisbe." In the Folio, Lysander reads the list of entertainments to Theseus, and Egeus advises against "Pyramus and Thisbe." The Folio thus incorporates Hermia's father into the wedding celebration. Since Egeus had bitterly opposed Hermia's marriage to Lysander, the Folio version of this scene requires the actor playing Egeus to decide what attitude to take toward Theseus, Lysander, and Hermia, who in both versions remains silent throughout.

3   *abridgement*

Diversion; pastime (i.e., an entertainment that will abridge or shorten the evening, though possibly the more familiar meaning, "a shortened version of a longer work," is intended)

More witnesseth than fancy's images   25
And grows to something of great constancy,
But, howsoever, strange and admirable. [1]

> *Enter lovers:* **Lysander**, **Demetrius**, **Hermia**, *and*
> **Helena**.

Theseus
Here come the lovers, full of joy and mirth.
—Joy, gentle friends! Joy and fresh days of love
Accompany your hearts!
Lysander
                              More than to us   30
table Wait in your royal walks, your board,° your bed!
Theseus
Come now, what masques, what dances shall we have
To wear away this long age of three hours
Between our after-supper and bedtime?
Where is our usual manager of mirth?   35
What revels are in hand? Is there no play
To ease the anguish of a torturing hour?
Call Philostrate.
Philostrate [2]
                              Here, mighty Theseus.
Theseus
Say, what abridgement [3] have you for this evening?
wile away What masque, what music? How shall we beguile°   40
slowly passing The lazy ° time if not with some delight?
Philostrate
list [*giving* **Theseus** *a paper*] There is a brief ° how many
entertainments / ready   sports° are ripe.°
Make choice of which your Highness will see first.

1 *The Battle with the Centaurs*

The legendary Hercules won a famous victory against the Centaurs (mythical creatures half man, half horse); Theseus, Hercules' cousin, also took part in the battle. The story is recounted in Ovid's *Metamorphoses* (Book 12).

2 *That have I told my love*

I have already told my love that story.

3 *The Riot of the Tipsy Bacchanals, / Tearing the Thracian Singer in their Rage.*

In Ovid's *Metamorphoses* (Book 11), the *Thracian singer* Orpheus was torn to pieces by the *Bacchanals* (*Bacchantes* in Ovid), frenzied and drunken women who worshipped Bacchus, the god of wine.

4 *The Thrice Three Muses Mourning for the Death / Of Learning*

Satires lamenting the decline of scholarship were popular in Shakespeare's day. The nine Muses were goddesses, each presiding over a different branch of learning.

5 *sorting with*

Suitable for

6 *A Tedious Brief Scene of Young Pyramus / And his Love Thisbe: Very Tragical Mirth.*

(See LONGER NOTE on page 232.)

Theseus

[*reads*] "The Battle with the Centaurs,¹ to be sung

By an Athenian eunuch to the harp."   45

have none   We'll none° of that. That have I told my love,²

In glory of my kinsman Hercules.

[*reads*] "The Riot of the Tipsy Bacchanals,

Tearing the Thracian Singer in their Rage."³

play   That is an old device,° and it was played   50

When I from Thebes came last a conqueror.

[*reads*] "The Thrice Three Muses Mourning for the Death

Of Learning,⁴ Late Deceased in Beggary."

That is some satire, keen and critical,

Not sorting with⁵ a nuptial ceremony.   55

[*reads*] "A Tedious Brief Scene of Young Pyramus

And his Love Thisbe: Very Tragical Mirth."⁶

"Merry" and "Tragical"? "Tedious" and "Brief"?

That is hot ice and wondrous strange snow.

How shall we find the concord of this discord?   60

Philostrate

A play there is, my lord, some ten words long,

Which is as "brief" as I have known a play.

But by ten words, my lord, it is too long,

Which makes it "tedious." For in all the play

well-cast   There is not one word apt, one player fitted;°   65

And "tragical," my noble lord, it is,

For Pyramus therein doth kill himself,

Which, when I saw rehearsed, I must confess,

Made mine eyes water—but more merry tears

The passion of loud laughter never shed.   70

Theseus

What are they that do play it?

Philostrate

Hard-handed men that work in Athens here,

1   *Extremely stretched and conned with*
    cruel pain

    **Overtaxed and learned with
    painful effort**

2   *wretchedness o'ercharged*

    Poor people overburdened

3   *duty in his service perishing*

    **I.e., exhausting themselves trying
    to perform their duty**

4   *noble respect / Takes it in might, not*
    merit

    **A generous judgment considers
    the ability of the doer rather than
    only the value of what is done.**

who / with   Which° never labored in° their minds till now,

strained / unpracticed   And now have toiled° their unbreathed° memories

in preparation for   With this same play against° your nuptial.   75

Theseus

And we will hear it.

Philostrate

         No, my noble lord.

It is not for you. I have heard it over,

And it is nothing, nothing in the world—

Unless you can find sport in their intents,

Extremely stretched and conned with cruel pain, [1]   80

To do you service.

Theseus

         I will hear that play,

For never anything can be amiss

sincerity   When simpleness° and duty tender it.

Go, bring them in.—And take your places, ladies.

                         [**Philostrate** exits.]

Hippolyta

I love not to see wretchedness o'ercharged, [2]   85

its   And duty in his° service perishing. [3]

Theseus

Why, gentle sweet, you shall see no such thing.

Hippolyta

He says they can do nothing in this kind.

Theseus

The kinder we, to give them thanks for nothing.

Our sport shall be to take what they mistake,   90

consideration   And what poor duty cannot do, noble respect°

Takes it in might, not merit. [4]

scholars / intended   Where I have come, great clerks° have purposèd°

To greet me with premeditated welcomes,

1 *Throttle their practiced accent*

Be unable to speak in the manner they rehearsed

2 *Out of this silence yet I picked a welcome, / And in the modesty of fearful duty / I read as much as from the rattling tongue / Of saucy and audacious eloquence*

Theseus appreciates the sincerity and humility of the stumbling, halting words of welcome spoken in *fearful duty* (i.e., nervous loyalty) as much as the fluent speeches he hears from more confident and eloquent speakers.

3 **Quince**

Quince recites his prologue with incorrect punctuation (see line 96, where Theseus anticipates this), making it say the opposite of what he intends.

4 *show*

Appearance (although it could possibly mean "dumbshow," a miming of the action of their play)

Where I have seen them shiver and look pale, 95

Make periods in the midst of sentences,

Throttle their practiced accent[1] in their fears,

silently And in conclusion dumbly° have broke off,

Not paying me a welcome. Trust me, sweet,

Out of this silence yet I picked a welcome, 100

And in the modesty of fearful duty

I read as much as from the rattling tongue

Of saucy and audacious eloquence.[2]

Love, therefore, and tongue-tied simplicity

mind In least speak most, to my capacity.° 105

[*Enter* **Philostrate**.]

Philostrate

ready So please your Grace, the Prologue is addressed.°

Theseus

Let him approach.

Enter [**Quince** *as*] *the Prologue.*

Quince [3]

[*as Prologue*] If we offend, it is with our good will.

That you should think we come not to offend

But with good will. To show our simple skill, 110

That is the true beginning of our end.

Consider then we come but in despite.

intending We do not come as minding° to content you,

Our true intent is. All for your delight

We are not here. That you should here repent you 115

The actors are at hand, and, by their show,[4]

You shall know all that you are like to know.

1   *stand upon points*

    Both "stand on ceremony" and
    "mind his punctuation" (*points* can
    mean "punctuation marks")

2   *He knows not the stop.*

    "He doesn't know how to stop it"
    (the *colt*), and "he doesn't
    recognize a period."

3   *think no scorn*

    Consider it no disgrace

Theseus

This fellow doth not stand upon points. [1]

Lysander

ridden (handled) / unbroken He hath rid° his prologue like a rough° colt. He knows

not the stop. [2] A good moral, my lord: it is not enough 120

to speak, but to speak true.

Hippolyta

Indeed he hath played on this prologue like a child on a

control recorder: a sound, but not in government.°

Theseus

His speech was like a tangled chain: nothing

damaged impaired,° but all disordered. Who is next? 125

Enter [**Bottom** *as*] Pyramus, *and* [**Flute** *as*] Thisbe, *and*
[**Snout** *as*] Wall, *and* [**Starveling** *as*] Moonshine, *and*
[**Snug** *as*] Lion.

Quince

perhaps [*as Prologue*] Gentles, perchance° you wonder at this

show,

But wonder on, till truth make all things plain.

This man is Pyramus, if you would know.

certainly This beauteous lady Thisbe is, certain.°

This man, with lime and roughcast, doth present 130

Wall, that vile wall which did these lovers sunder,

And through Wall's chink, poor souls, they are content

To whisper—at the which let no man wonder.

This man, with lantern, dog, and bush of thorn,

Presenteth Moonshine. For, if you will know, 135

By moonshine did these lovers think no scorn [3]

To meet at Ninus' tomb—there, there to woo.

1   *broached*

   Stabbed, but could also mean
   "tapped," as a keg of beer is tapped
   to let the beer flow.

2   *At large discourse*

   Speak at length

3   *lime and hair*

   I.e., a wall (*lime* and *hair* being two
   of the wall's materials, *hair* being
   used to bind the plaster)

is called This grisly beast, which "Lion" hight° by name,

The trusty Thisbe, coming first by night,

frighten Did scare away or, rather, did affright;°   140

cloak / drop And, as she fled, her mantle° she did fall,°

Which Lion vile with bloody mouth did stain.

Soon / brave Anon° comes Pyramus, sweet youth and tall,°

And finds his trusty Thisbe's mantle slain;

Whereat, with blade, with bloody blameful blade,   145

He bravely broached¹ his boiling bloody breast,

waiting And Thisbe, tarrying° in mulberry shade,

His dagger drew and died. For all the rest,

Let Lion, Moonshine, Wall, and lovers twain

At large discourse,² while here they do remain.   150

Theseus

is I wonder if the lion be° to speak.

Demetrius

No wonder, my lord: one lion may when many asses do.

[*All the mechanicals exit, except for* **Snout** *as Wall.*]

Snout

play [*as Wall*] In this same interlude° it doth befall

That I, one Snout by name, present a wall;

And such a wall, as I would have you think,   155

That had in it a crannied hole, or chink,

Through which the lovers, Pyramus and Thisbe,

Did whisper often very secretly.

This loam, this roughcast, and this stone doth show

That I am that same wall. The truth is so.   160

left And this the cranny is, right and sinister,°

Through which the fearful lovers are to whisper.

Theseus

Would you desire lime and hair³ to speak better?

1　*which ever art*

　Which always is

2　*Show me thy chink*

　Many editors and directors assume
　that Snout indicates the chink in
　the wall by forming a V with his
　fingers, as Bottom suggested he
　might do at their rehearsal (*[o]r let
　him hold his fingers thus* [3.1.60–61]).
　However, if Snout creates the chink
　by spreading his legs, the scene's
　potential hilarity can be fully
　realized, as can its ironic
　fulfillment of Bottom's earlier
　malapropistic desire to perform
　obscenely (1.2.94). The obscene
　staging is supported by puns on
　the hairy *stones* (testicles) and *hole*
　(anus) that Thisbe kisses instead of
　her lover's lips (187, 198).

3　*Jove*

　King of the gods (Roman)

Demetrius

It is the wittiest partition that ever I heard discourse,
my lord.   165

[*Enter* **Bottom** *as Pyramus.*]

Theseus

Pyramus draws near the wall. Silence!

Bottom

grim-looking [*as Pyramus*] O grim-looked° night! O night with hue so
black!

O night, which ever art¹ when day is not!

O night, O night! Alack, alack, alack,

I fear my Thisbe's promise is forgot!   170

—And thou, O Wall, O sweet, O lovely Wall,

That stand'st between her father's ground and mine,

Thou Wall, O Wall, O sweet and lovely Wall,

eyes Show me thy chink² to blink through with mine eyne!°

[**Snout** *reveals the chink.*]

Thanks, courteous Wall. Jove³ shield thee well for this!   175

But what see I? No Thisbe do I see.

O wicked Wall, through whom I see no bliss,

Cursed be thy stones for thus deceiving me!

Theseus

capable of feeling The wall, methinks, being sensible,° should curse

in response again.°   180

Bottom

[*to* **Theseus**] No, in truth, sir, he should not. "Deceiving me" is Thisbe's cue. She is to enter now, and I am to
exactly spy her through the wall. You shall see, it will fall pat°
as I told you. Yonder she comes.

Enter [**Flute** *as*] *Thisbe.*

1 *Limander*

Bottom means *Leander*, a famous lover in Greek myth, who drowned trying to swim the Hellespont to reach Hero.

2 *Helen*

Flute may be thinking of Helen of Troy, but Leander's love was named Hero. The mention of Helen, who was forced to leave her husband for the Trojan Prince Paris (the event that began the Trojan War), is an unnerving reference for an assertion of true love.

3 *the Fates*

Three sister goddesses in classical mythology, who controlled individuals' fates by spinning, weaving, and cutting the threads that determined their destinies.

4 *Shafalus to Procrus*

Bottom means "Cephalus to Procris," another famous pair of Greek lovers (though Cephalus, who remained faithful to his wife after he was abducted by Aurora, later accused Procris of infidelity, as she in turn accused him—and was accidently slain by him. See Ovid's *Metamorphoses*, Book 7).

5 *Tide life, tide death*

I.e., come life or death (*tide* meaning "betide," or "happen")

Flute

[*as Thisbe*] O Wall, full often hast thou heard my moans   185
For parting my fair Pyramus and me!
My cherry lips have often kissed thy stones,
Thy stones with lime and hair knit up in thee.

Bottom

[*as Pyramus*] I see a voice. Now will I to the chink
if   To spy an° I can hear my Thisbe's face. Thisbe?   190

Flute

[*as Thisbe*] My love! Thou art, my love, I think.

Bottom

[*as Pyramus*] Think what thou wilt. I am thy lover's grace,
And like Limander¹ am I trusty still.

Flute

[*as Thisbe*] And I like Helen,² till the Fates³ me kill.

Bottom

[*as Pyramus*] Not Shafalus to Procrus⁴ was so true.   195

Flute

[*as Thisbe*] As Shafalus to Procrus, I to you.

Bottom

[*as Pyramus*] Oh, kiss me through the hole of this vile
wall!

Flute

[*as Thisbe*] I kiss the wall's hole, not your lips at all.

Bottom

[*as Pyramus*] Wilt thou at Ninny's tomb meet me
straightway?

Flute

[*as Thisbe*] Tide life, tide death,⁵ I come without delay.   200

                    [**Bottom** *and* **Flute** *exit.*]

Snout

recited   [*as Wall*] Thus have I, Wall, my part dischargèd° so,

1   *without warning*

    I.e., without warning Pyramus's
    and Thisbe's parents

2   *shadows*

    I.e., reflections of the reality they
    represent

3   *nor else no lion's dam*

    I.e., but in no other way (than in
    this role) has he given birth to a
    lion (*dam* = mother)

4   *in strife*

    Violently

5   *'twere pity on*

    It would be risking

And, being done, thus Wall away doth go.   [*He exits.*]

Theseus

wall   Now is the mural° down between the two neighbors.

Demetrius

No remedy, my lord, when walls are so willful to hear

without warning. [1]   205

Hippolyta

This is the silliest stuff that ever I heard.

Theseus

profession (i.e., actors)   The best in this kind° are but shadows, [2] and the worst

are no worse if imagination amend them.

Hippolyta

It must be your imagination, then, and not theirs.

Theseus

If we imagine no worse of them than they of them-   210

selves, they may pass for excellent men. Here come

two noble beasts in: a man and a lion.

Enter [**Snug** *as*] *Lion and* [**Starveling** *as*] *Moonshine,*
[*with a lantern, thornbush, and dog*].

Snug

[*as Lion*] You ladies, you whose gentle hearts do fear

The smallest monstrous mouse that creeps on floor,

May now perchance both quake and tremble here,   215

When Lion rough in wildest rage doth roar.

Then know that I, as Snug the joiner, am

savage   A lion fell,° nor else no lion's dam. [3]

For if I should as Lion come in strife [4]

Into this place, 'twere pity on my life. [5]   220

Theseus

A very gentle beast and of a good conscience.

1 *a very fox for his valor*

I.e., not brave; foxes were known for their cunning, but not for their courage.

2 *goose*

A proverbially foolish animal

3 *He should have worn the horns on his head.*

Referring to a conventional notion that cuckolds (men whose wives had been unfaithful) grew horns on their heads

4 *in snuff*

Both "needing to be snuffed out" and "angry." Starveling is visibly angry at the interruptions.

Demetrius

The very best at a beast, my lord, that e'er I saw.

Lysander

This lion is a very fox for his valor. [1]

Theseus

True, and a goose [2] for his discretion.

Demetrius

Not so, my lord, for his valor cannot carry his discre-   225
tion, and the fox carries the goose.

Theseus

His discretion, I am sure, cannot carry his valor, for
the goose carries not the fox. It is well. Leave it to his
discretion, and let us listen to the moon.

Starveling

crescent   [*as Moonshine*] This lantern doth the hornèd° moon
         present—   230

Demetrius

He should have worn the horns on his head. [3]

Theseus

crescent moon   He is no crescent,° and his horns are invisible within
the circumference.

Starveling

[*as Moonshine*] This lantern doth the hornèd moon
         present.

Myself the man i' th' moon do seem to be—   235

Theseus

This is the greatest error of all the rest. The man should
be put into the lantern. How is it else the "man i' th'
moon"?

Demetrius

for fear of   He dares not come there for° the candle, for you see, it is
already in snuff. [4]   240

1   *in the wane*
    In decline (referring to the
    decrease of the visible portion of
    the moon as it completes its cycle)

2   *moused*
    I.e., grabbed in the mouth and
    shaken, like a cat with a mouse

Hippolyta

I wish   I am aweary of this moon. Would° he would change!

Theseus

It appears by his small light of discretion that he is in
the wane.[1] But yet, in courtesy, in all reason, we must
wait out   stay° the time.

Lysander

Proceed, Moon.   245

Starveling

All that I have to say is to tell you that the lantern is the
moon; I, the man i'th' moon; this thornbush, my
thornbush; and this dog, my dog.

Demetrius

Why, all these should be in the lantern, for all these are
in the moon.—But silence! Here comes Thisbe.   250

Enter [**Flute** *as*] *Thisbe.*

Flute

[*as Thisbe*] This is old Ninny's tomb. Where is my love?

Snug

[*as Lion, roaring*] Oh!   [**Flute** *runs off, dropping her mantle.*]

Demetrius

Well roared, Lion!

Theseus

Well run, Thisbe!

Hippolyta

Well shone, Moon!—Truly, the moon shines with a   255
good grace.   [*Lion gnaws on Thisbe's mantle.*]

Theseus

Well moused,[2] Lion!

1 *Furies*

   Greek goddesses who took
   revenge on those who were guilty
   of crimes

2 *thrum*

   The small piece of thread left on
   the loom after the woven material
   is cut. The image follows from the
   reference to the *Fates* (see line 194
   and note), but Bottom, of course,
   is a weaver.

3 *go near*

   Do much

*Enter [**Bottom** as] Pyramus.*

Demetrius

And then came Pyramus.   [**Snug** exits.]

Lysander

And so the lion vanished.

Bottom

[*as Pyramus*]Sweet Moon, I thank thee for thy sunny

    beams.   260

I thank thee, Moon, for shining now so bright,

For by thy gracious, golden, glittering gleams,

I trust to take of truest Thisbe sight.

But stay! O spite!

look   But mark,° poor knight,   265

sorrow   What dreadful dole° is here!

Eyes, do you see?

How can it be?

O dainty duck! O dear!

Thy mantle good—   270

What? Stained with blood?

cruel   Approach, ye Furies¹ fell!°

O Fates, come, come,

Cut thread and thrum,²

Destroy / kill Quail,° crush, conclude, and quell!°   275

Theseus

emotional display This passion,° and the death of a dear friend, would

go near³ to make a man look sad.

Hippolyta

Curse   Beshrew° my heart, but I pity the man.

Bottom

why   [*as Pyramus*] O wherefore,° Nature, didst thou lions

create   frame,°

1   *deflowered*

    **Bottom means "devoured"
    (*deflowered* means "took her
    virginity")**

2   *No die, but an ace*

    **Demetrius puns on *die* meaning
    "one of a pair of dice," with *ace*
    meaning the side with the single
    spot.**

3   *ass*

    Theseus puns on "ace."

4   *How chance*

    How is it that

Since lion vile hath here deflowered [1] my dear, 280

Who Which° is—no, no—which was the fairest dame

That lived, that loved, that liked, that looked with cheer?

destroy Come, tears, confound!°

Out, sword, and wound!

breast The pap° of Pyramus— 285

Ay, that left pap

Where heart doth hop.

[stabbing himself] Thus die I, thus, thus, thus.

Now am I dead.

Now am I fled. 290

My soul is in the sky.

Tongue, lose thy light.

Moon, take thy flight.   [**Starveling** exits.]

Now die, die, die, die, die.   [pretends to die]

Demetrius

No die, but an ace [2] for him, for he is but one. 295

Lysander

Less than an ace, man, for he is dead. He is nothing.

Theseus

With the help of a surgeon he might yet recover and yet

prove an ass. [3]

Hippolyta

How chance [4] Moonshine is gone before Thisbe comes

back and finds her lover? 300

Theseus

She will find him by starlight. Here she comes, and her

passion ends the play.

[Enter **Flute** as Thisbe.]

1   *means*

    (1) laments; (2) objects; protests

2   *Sisters three*

    The Fates (see line 194 and note)

Hippolyta

Methinks she should not use a long one for such a
Pyramus. I hope she will be brief.

Demetrius

speck　　　A mote° will turn the balance, which Pyramus, which　　305
preserve　　Thisbe, is the better. He for a man, God warrant° us; she
　　　　　　for a woman, God bless us.

Lysander

She hath spied him already with those sweet eyes.

Demetrius

as you will see　　And thus she means, [1] *videlicet*°—

Flute

[*as Thisbe*] Asleep, my love?　　　　　　　　　　　　　310
What, dead, my dove?
O Pyramus, arise!
Speak, speak. Quite dumb?
Dead, dead? A tomb
Must cover thy sweet eyes.　　　　　　　　　　　　　315
These lily lips,
This cherry nose,
These yellow cowslip cheeks
Are gone, are gone.
Lovers, make moan.　　　　　　　　　　　　　　　320
His eyes were green as leeks.
O Sisters three, [2]
Come, come to me
With hands as pale as milk.
Lay them in gore,　　　　　　　　　　　　　　　　325
cut; shorn　　Since you have shore°
With shears his thread of silk.
Tongue, not a word.
Come, trusty sword.

1   *bergomask dance*

An Italian country dance (from
Bergamo, a city in northern Italy)

2   *iron tongue*

I.e., the clapper in a clock bell

3   *told*

Counted (*told* is suggested by
tongue, and is an inaudible pun on
the more usual "tolled")

4   *fairy time*

I.e., late at night when the fairies
appear; Theseus's earlier
skepticism about *fairy toys* (5.1.3)
suggests that this is for him either
a joke or a familiar cliché; the play,
however, reveals it to be an
unwitting acknowledgment of a
world beyond the human realm.

5   *heavy gait*

Wearying passage

6   *A fortnight hold we this solemnity*

We will continue this celebration
for two weeks.

stain Come, blade, my breast imbrue.° [*stabs herself*] 330

And, farewell, friends.

Thus Thisbe ends.

Adieu, adieu, adieu. [*pretends to die*]

Theseus

Moonshine and Lion are left to bury the dead.

Demetrius

Ay, and Wall too. 335

Bottom

No, I assure you. The wall is down that parted their

fathers. Will it please you to see the epilogue, or to

hear a bergomask dance[1] between two of our company?

Theseus

No epilogue, I pray you, for your play needs no excuse.

Never excuse: for when the players are all dead, there 340

need none to be blamed. Marry, if he that writ it had

played Pyramus and hanged himself in Thisbe's garter,

it would have been a fine tragedy—and so it is, truly,

performed and very notably discharged.° But come, your bergo-

mask. Let your epilogue alone. 345

[**Bottom** *and* **Flute** *stand, dance, and then*

all the mechanicals exit.]

The iron tongue[2] of midnight hath told[3] twelve.

Lovers, to bed. 'Tis almost fairy time.[4]

I fear we shall outsleep the coming morn

stayed awake As much as we this night have overwatched.°

obviously crude This palpable-gross° play hath well beguiled 350

The heavy gait[5] of night. Sweet friends, to bed.

A fortnight hold we this solemnity,[6]

In nightly revels and new jollity. *They exit.*

Enter [**Robin**].

1   *wasted brands*

Dying embers

2   *In remembrance of a shroud*

I.e., in mind of his death (*shroud* is the cloth in which the body is wrapped for burial)

3   *his sprite*

Its ghost

4   *triple Hecate's team*

The team of dragons pulling Hecate's chariot. The Greek goddess of night, Hecate, (pronounced with two syllables, HECK-it), took three separate forms: as Cynthia (or Luna) in the sky; as Diana on Earth; and as Proserpina in the underworld.

5   *I am sent with broom*

The broom was a traditional attribute of the folk figure of Robin Goodfellow, who was sometimes credited with cleaning houses while their owners slept.

Robin

Now the hungry lion roars,

howls at   And the wolf behowls° the moon,   355

tired   Whilst the heavy° ploughman snores,

exhausted   All with weary task fordone.°

Now the wasted brands¹ do glow

Whilst the screech-owl, screeching loud,

Puts the wretch that lies in woe   360

In remembrance of a shroud.²

Now it is the time of night

That the graves, all gaping wide,

Every one lets forth his sprite³

In the churchway paths to glide.   365

And we fairies, that do run

By the triple Hecate's team⁴

From the presence of the sun,

Following darkness like a dream,

joyful   Now are frolic.° Not a mouse   370

Shall disturb this hallowed house.

I am sent with broom⁵ before

To sweep the dust behind the door.

*Enter [**Oberon** and **Titania**] King and Queen of Fairies,
with all their train.*

Oberon

Through the house give glimmering light;

By the dead and drowsy fire   375

Every elf and fairy sprite

Hop as light as bird from brier,

And this ditty, after me,

Sing, and dance it trippingly.

1   *best bride bed*

    I.e., Theseus and Hippolyta's

2   *And the blots of nature's hand / Shall not*
    in their issue stand. / Never mole, harelip,
    nor scar, / Nor mark prodigious, such as
    are / Despisèd in nativity, / Shall upon
    their children be.

    The fairies' blessing intends to
    banish the possibility that the
    children (*issue*) of these newly
    wedded couples might suffer un-
    natural deformities. This evident
    anxiety about the possibility of
    deformed or unnatural births can
    be understood in part as a
    response to the bestiality hinted at
    in Titania's encounter with
    Bottom, since it was believed that
    interspecies intercourse could
    produce hybrid monsters. In Ovid's
    ***Metamorphoses* (Book 8), Pasiphaë's**
    intercourse with a bull produces
    the Minotaur, a monster with the
    body of a man and the head of a
    bull. Theseus kills the Minotaur
    and escapes from the labyrinth in
    which the monster was kept with
    the help of Ariadne, whom Oberon
    names as one of the women
    betrayed by Theseus (2.1.80).

3   *field dew consecrate*

    Consecrated *field dew* (i.e., the fairy
    equivalent of holy water)

Titania

repeat	First, rehearse° your song by rote,	380

To each word a warbling note.
Hand in hand with fairy grace
Will we sing and bless this place.

[*The* **Fairies** *sing and dance.*]

Oberon

[*sings*] Now until the break of day
Through this house each fairy stray. 385
To the best bride bed¹ will we,
Which by us shall blessèd be,

children And the issue° there create
Ever shall be fortunate.
So shall all the couples three 390
Ever true in loving be,
And the blots of nature's hand
Shall not in their issue stand.
Never mole, harelip, nor scar,

abnormal Nor mark prodigious,° such as are 395
Despisèd in nativity,
Shall upon their children be.²
With this field dew consecrate,³

way Every fairy take his gait,°
separate And each several° chamber bless 400
Through this palace with sweet peace,
And the owner of it blessed
Ever shall in safety rest.
Trip away. Make no stay.
Meet me all by break of day. 405

They exit [*but* **Robin** *remains*].

1   *shadows*

Robin has called Oberon *King of
shadows* (3.2.347), where its primary
meaning is "spirits" (see note 4 on
p. 156), and Theseus uses the term
in relation to the acting by the
mechanicals in 5.1.207. Here,
Robin in character uses the term to
define his fairy nature, but as the
speaker of what is the play's
epilogue it inevitably takes on its
familiar sense of "actor."

2   *No more yielding but a dream*

Yielding no more (meaning) than a
dream does

3   *'scape the serpent's tongue*

I.e., avoid being hissed by the
audience

4   *Give me your hands*

Applaud us

5   *restore amends*

Give delight in return

Robin

If we shadows[1] have offended,

only Think but° this, and all is mended:

That you have but slumbered here

While these visions did appear.

foolish And this weak and idle° theme,   410

No more yielding but a dream,[2]

Gentles, do not reprehend.

If you pardon, we will mend.

And, as I am an honest puck,

If we have unearnèd luck   415

Now to 'scape the serpent's tongue,[3]

We will make amends ere long.

Otherwise Else° the puck a liar call.

So good night unto you all.

Give me your hands[4] if we be friends,   420

And Robin shall restore amends.[5]   [*He exits.*]

Longer Notes

PAGE 45

1.1.9–10   *like to a silver bow / Now bent in Heaven*

In all of the early printings of the play, Hippolyta refers as here to the moon as a silver bow "Now bent in Heaven." Hippolyta's description of the current moon as a bent silver bow appears to contradict Theseus's negative description of the waning moon as a withered old widow. Hence many modern editions follow Nicholas Rowe, an 18th-century editor of Shakespeare, in changing "Now bent" to "New bent." With this change, Hippolyta anticipates that on their wedding night the new crescent moon will shine like a silver bow. However, the original reading makes perfect sense. The play does not provide a clear indication of Hippolyta's attitude toward her impending marriage. If, however, we regard Hippolyta as an Amazon war bride anxious about the end of her independent existence, her favorable image of the waning moon that delays the arrival of her wedding night is understandable. Moreover, her comparison of the moon to a silver bow might allude to the fabled military prowess of Amazon warriors; legend had it that Amazons burned off their right breasts in order to accommodate their bows. The four days that Theseus perceives as passing with tortuous slowness perhaps pass all too quickly for Hippolyta. For this and some other thinking about the text of the play, I am indebted to Patricia Parker.

PAGE 49

1.1.70–73   *You can endure the livery
of a nun, / For aye to be in shady cloister
mewed / To live a barren sister all your
life, / Chanting faint hymns to the cold,
fruitless moon*

Theseus sees the life of a nun as a
withdrawal from life, marked by
a barreness like that of the *cold,
fruitless moon* (Diana, goddess of
the moon, was also the goddess
of chastity). Although Theseus
depicts life in the cloister as
anemically spare, convents had
once provided English women
with a respectable way to lead
unmarried lives. Following
the Protestant Reformation in
England, all Catholic convents
and monasteries were dissolved
between 1536 and 1539. Unlike
Catholics, who regarded virginity
as the superior spiritual condition, Protestants placed greater
emphasis on marital chastity
(sexual self-restraint and fidelity
between spouses). According to
Protestant doctrine, marriage
was instituted of God for the
reproduction of children and to
provide fellowship between men
and women.

PAGES 79 AND 81

2.1.77–80   *Didst thou not lead him
through the glimmering night / From
Perigenia, whom he ravishèd? / And
make him with fair Aegles break his
faith, / With Ariadne and Antiopa?*

The Theseus legend was available to Shakespeare in Thomas
North's translation of *The Lives
of the Noble Greeks and Romans*
(1579), written by the ancient
Roman writer Plutarch. Plutarch
recounts how Theseus ravished
and broke his faith with women
such as Perigenia (or Perigouna,
as it is in North), Ariadne, and
Antiope. Oberon's claim that
Titania assisted Theseus in these
dishonorable acts is Shakespeare's (and perhaps Oberon's)
invention.

PAGE 197

5.1.56–57   *A Tedious Brief Scene of
Young Pyramus / And his Love Thisbe:
Very Tragical Mirth.*

Why does Theseus choose
Pyramus and Thisbe over the other
three entertainments? Theseus
claims that he rejects the alternatives on the grounds that he
already knows the story, that he

has seen the play before, or that the subject is inappropriate for a wedding. Yet he might also wish to avoid the airing of awkward or alarming subjects in these particular entertainments. Theseus participated in the battle with the Centaurs, which violently disrupted a wedding celebration; moreover, the eunuch who sings this tale uncomfortably recalls the fabled Amazonian practice of castrating boys and putting them to work at typically feminine domestic tasks. The play about the tipsy Bacchanals, drunken followers of the god Bacchus who dismembered the poet Orpheus, might too overtly depict female aggression against the male body. Theseus rejects the third play, the nine *Muses Mourning for the Death / Of Learning, Late Deceased in Beggary*, as an evident satire on the lack of financial patronage available to Athenian poets. This play appears to have a political agenda: to use *the rattling tongue / Of saucy and audacious eloquence* to shame the Duke into becoming

a more supportive patron of the arts (5.1.102–103). Having just dismissed poets as fabricators of airy nothing, Theseus is unlikely to sympathize with the plight of poor intellectuals. However, like the battle with the Centaurs and the rage of the Bacchanals, the Ovidian story of suicidal lovers depicted in *Pyramus and Thisbe* itself hardly seems appropriate for a wedding celebration. In contrast to the other offerings, however, the artisans' play might appeal to Theseus as a palpably amateur production intended only to do him *service* (5.1.81).

A
MIDSOMMER NIGHTS
DREAME.

Enter Theseus, Hippolita, *with others.*

Theseus.

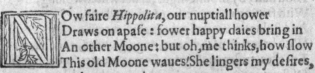

Ow faire *Hippolita*, our nuptiall hower
Draws on apase : fower happy daies bring in
An other Moone: but oh, me thinks, how flow
This old Moone waues! She lingers my defires,
Like to a Stepdame, or a dowager,
Long withering out a yong mans reuenewe.

Hip. Fower daies will quickly fteepe themfelues in night:
Fower nights will quickly dreame away the time:
And then the Moone, like to a filuer bowe,
Now bent in heauen, fhall beholde the night
Of our folemnities.

The. Goe *Philoftrate*,
Stirre vp the *Athenian* youth to merriments,
Awake the peart and nimble spirit of mirth,
Turne melancholy foorth ro funerals:
The pale companion is not for our pomp.
Hyppolita, I woo'd thee with my fword,
And wonne thy loue, doing thee iniuries:
But I will wed thee in another key,
With pompe, with triumph, and with reueling.

    Enter Egeus *and his daughter* Hermia, *and* Lyfander
    and Helena, *and* Demetrius.

Ege. Happy be *Thefeus*, our renowned duke.
The. Thankes good *Egeus*. Whats the newes with thee?
Ege. Full of vexation, come I, with complaint

A reproduction of the first page of *A Midsummer Night's Dream* in the First Quarto (1600).

Editing *A Midsummer Night's Dream*
by David Scott Kastan

Midsummer Night's Dream was first printed in 1600 in a small quarto edition (Q1) published by Thomas Fisher. The title page of this edition says that the play had been "sundry times" played by Shakespeare's company by the time it appeared in print. It is a well-printed text, seemingly derived from a draft, most likely written in Shakespeare's own hand, but one that had not yet worked out the specific demands of performance. A substantial number of necessary exits and entrances are unmarked, and certain phrases, like "with others," which appears in the play's first entry direction, would be good enough for an author imagining the opening entrance but would not serve the needs of actors who must know exactly how many of them are necessary to appear on stage. A second edition (Q2), essentially a reprint of the first, appeared in 1619 (although with a title page dated 1600, most likely to obscure the fact that the effort of the publisher, Thomas Pavier, to publish this and nine other plays by Shakespeare had been prohibited following an appeal of the acting company, then the King's Men, to the government). The play appeared again in the Folio published in 1623, as the eighth play in the section of comedies. It was set from a copy of Q2 but apparently checked and sometimes revised with reference to what seems to have been a copy marked for use in the theater. It makes a number of changes and additions, mainly affecting stage directions, as well as introducing about fifty minor errors on top of the fifty or so it carried over from Q2. The first edition is, therefore, closest to what Shakespeare initially wrote, and it is the one on which this present edition is based.

In general, the editorial work of this present edition is conservative, a matter of normalizing spelling, capitalization, and punctuation, removing superfluous italics, regularizing the names of characters, and rationalizing entrances and exits. Emendations are made only when the reading of Q1 seems manifestly wrong. A comparison of the edited text of 1.1.1–22 with the facsimile page of the Quarto (on p. 234) reveals some of the issues in this process. The speech prefixes are expanded and normalized for clarity, so that *Hip.* and *The.* become Hippolyta and Theseus. Spelling, capitalization, and italicization here regularly follow modern practices rather than the habits of the Quarto's printers. As neither spelling nor punctuation in Shakespeare's time had yet been standardized, words were spelled in various ways that indicated their proximate pronunciation, and punctuation, which then was largely a rhythmical pointer rather than predominantly designed, as it is now, to clarify logical relations, was necessarily far more idiosyncratic than today. In any case, compositors were under no obligation to follow either the spelling or punctuation of their copy. For most readers, then, there is little advantage in an edition that reproduces the spelling and punctuation of the Quarto text. It does not accurately represent Shakespeare's writing habits, and it makes reading difficult, in a way Shakespeare could never have anticipated or desired.

Therefore "MIDSOMMER" in the title here everywhere becomes *Midsummer*, "NIGHTS" becomes *Nights*, and "DREAME" becomes *Dream*. In the first line of the play "hower" becomes the familiar "hour," as "fower" in line 2 becomes "four." In line 9 "siluer" becomes "silver," though it is interesting to note that "u" was then often used where we use a "v," as "i" could be used where we use a "j," as in "iniuries" in line 17. The intrusive "e"s in words like "faire" in line 1 or "Moone" in line 9 are eliminated, as is the "literary" capitalization of the noun. In line 4, however, something more than modernization is required: "waues" is not the modern "waves," but clearly "wanes," the error the result of the fact that "u" and "n" are each upside down versions of the other and easily confused in the printing process. The colons in lines 2 and 3 mark a heavy pause rather than define a precise grammatical relation as they would in modern usage, and in this text they are replaced with the periods that accord with modern practices. In all these cases, editing clarifies rather than alters Shakespeare's intentions. Thus, 1.1.1–4 reads in the Quarto:

NOW faire *Hippolita*, our nuptial hower
Draws on apase : fower happy daies bring in
An other Moone : but oh, me thinks, how slow
This old Moone waues!

Modernized and emended this reads:

Now fair Hippolyta, our nuptial hour
Draws on apace. Four happy days bring in
Another moon. But, oh, methinks how slow
This old moon wanes.

Though the emendation of "waues" to "wanes" clearly restores the intended word, admittedly the modernizations involve some loss. Clarity and consistency is gained at the expense of expressive detail, but normalizing spelling, capitalization, and punctuation allows the text to be read with far greater ease than the original, and essentially as it was intended to be understood. We lose the archaic feel of the text in exchange for clarity of meaning. Old spellings are consistently modernized in this edition, but old *forms* of words (e.g., "eyne" for "eyes" at 1.1.242) are retained. The superfluous italics of proper names or adjectives are removed (e.g. *Hippolita* in line 1, which is also rendered in its usual modern form, Hippolyta). Punctuation, too, is adjusted to reflect modern practice, so punctuation that was then largely rhythmical in its functioning articulates logical relations as it does in modern practice. If, inevitably, in such modernization we lose the historical feel of the text Shakespeare's contemporaries read, it is important to remember that Shakespeare's contemporaries would not have thought the book they read in any sense archaic or quaint, as these details inevitably make it for a reader today. The text would have seemed to them as modern as this one does to us.

Modern readers, however, cannot help but be distracted by the different conventions they encounter on the Quarto page. While it is indeed of interest to see how orthography and typography have changed over time, these changes are not primary concerns for most readers of this edition. What little, then, is lost in a careful modernization of the text is more than made up for by the removal of the artificial obstacle of unfamiliar spelling forms and punctuation habits, which Shakespeare never could have intended as interpretive difficulties for his readers.

Textual Notes

The list below records all substantive departures in this edition from the Quarto text of 1600 (Q1). It does not record modernizations of spelling, normalization in the use of capitals, corrections of obvious typographical errors, adjustments of lineation, minor repositioning of stage directions (SD), or rationalizations of speech prefixes (SP).

Act and scene designations, all absent from the Quarto, also are not recorded. The adopted reading in this edition is given first in boldface and followed by the original, rejected reading of Q1, or noted as being absent from the Quarto text. Editorial stage directions are not collated but are enclosed within brackets in the text. Latin stage directions are translated (e.g., *They all exit* for *Exeunt omnes*).

1.1.4 wanes waues; **1.1.19SD Lysander** Lysander and Helena; **1.1.24 Stand forth, Demetrius.** [Possibly intended as a stage direction in Q and F; it is printed in italics and centered on its own line.]; **1.1.26 Stand forth, Lysander.** [Possibly intended as a stage direction in Q and F; it is printed in italics and centered on its own line.]; **1.1.136 low** loue; **1.1.187 Yours would** Your words; **1.1.191 I'd** ile; **1.1.219 stranger companies** strange companions; **1.2.25–32 The raging rocks...The foolish Fates.** [Printed as prose in Q]

2.1.79 Aegles Eagles; **2.1.97 murrain** murrion; **2.1.101 cheer** heere; **2.1.109 thin** chinne; **2.1.154SP Robin (and throughout)** *Puck* (sometimes *Pu.*); **2.1.158 the west** west; **2.1.201, 202 not...nor** not, not; **2.2.9SP** [not in Q]; **2.2.13SP** [not in Q]; **2.2.24SP Fairies** 2. *Fai.*; **2.2.24–30 Philomel...with lullaby.** Philomele...with melody; **2.2.45 Be** Bet; **2.2.49 good** god; **2.2.53 is** it; **2.2.155 ate** eate

3.1.48SP Bottom *Cet.* ; **3.1.73 "Odious?" "Odors!"** Odours, odorous; **3.1 77SP Robin** *Quin.*; **3.1.83 bristly juvenile** brisky Iuuenall; **3.1.110 ouzel** Woosell; **3.1.134 own** owe; **3.1.146 Peaseblossom Ready. Cobweb And I. Mote And I. Mustardseed And I. All Where shall we go?** *Fairies.* Readie: and I, and I, and I. Where shall we goe?; **3.1.159SP Peaseblossom** 1. Fai.; **3.1.159 Hail, mortal.** Haile mortall, haile; **3.1.159SP Cobweb** [Not in Q]; **3.1.159 Hail.** [spoken by Cobweb here, displaced from first part of line]; **3.1.159SP Mote** 2. *Fai.*; **3.1.159SP Mustardseed**

3. Fai.; **3.1.176 of** [not in Q]; **3.1.181 love's** louers; **3.2.4SD Enter Robin Goodfellow.** Q places this at beginning of scene: *Enter King of* Fairies, *and Robin goodfellow.;* **3.2.19 mimic** Minnick; **3.2.80 so** [not in Q]; **3.2.85 sleep** slippe; **3.2.175 Lest** Least; **3.2.213 like** life; **3.2.215 rend** rent; **3.2.250 prayers** praise; **3.2.299 gentlemen** gentleman; **3.2.326 but** hut; **3.2.426 shalt** shat; **3.2.451 To** [not in Q]

4.1.0SD and Bottom *and Clowne;* **4.1.5SP Bottom** *Clown* [*Clow., Clo.,* throughout scene]; **4.1.72 o'er** or; **4.1.81 these five** these, fine; **4.1.82 ho!** howe; **4.1.95 the** [not in Q]; **4.1.116 Seemed** Seeme; **4.1.127 is** [not in Q]; **4.1.132 rite** right; **4.1.171 saw** see; **4.1.172 in** a; **4.1.198 let us** let's; **4.1.205 to** [not in Q]; **4.1.208 a patched** patcht a; **4.2.0SD Enter Quince, Flute, [Snout, and Starveling].** *Enter* Quince, Flute, Thisby *and the rabble.;* **4.2.3SP Starveling** *Flut.;* **4.2.4SP Flute** *Thys.* [*This.,* throughout scene]; **4.2.25 no** not

5.1.34 our or; **5.1.107SP Theseus** *Duk.;* **5.1.119 his** this; **5.1.154 Snout** Flute; **5.1.188 up in thee** nowagaine; **5.1.203SP Theseus** *Duk.* [through end of play]; **5.1.203 mural down** Moon vsed; **5.1.241SP Hippolyta** *Dutch.* [through end of play]; **5.1.262 gleams** beams; **5.1.305 mote** moth; **5.1.306 warrant** warnd; **5.1.336SP Bottom** *Lyon.;* **5.1.354SD Enter Robin** *Enter* Pucke; **5.1.354 lion** Lyons; **5.1.355 behowls** beholds; **5.1.402–403 And the owner of it blessed / Ever shall in safety rest.** Euer shall in safety rest, / And the owner of it blest

A Midsummer Night's Dream on the Early Stage
by Mario DiGangi

To imagine how *A Midsummer Night's Dream* might have looked on the Elizabethan stage, it is necessary to banish the vision of gauzily attired ballerina fairies dancing through a moonlit forest. Elizabethan playing companies did not have movable scenery, lighting effects, flight machines, authentic period costumes, or a large corps of dancers to represent a fairy-haunted wood or an Athenian court. Instead, they relied on symbolic costumes and properties, richly descriptive language, and, most of all, playgoers' willingness to use their imaginations.

The original performance of *A Midsummer Night's Dream* probably took place at The Theatre, one of the large open-air venues that Shakespeare's company used prior to the building of the Globe in 1596. Like the Globe, the Theatre was a three-story "round" (or multi-sided polygonal) structure surrounding a large rectangular stage approximately twenty-five feet deep by forty-five feet wide. At the back of the stage was the tiring ("attiring") house, a three-tiered structure that contained rooms for storing properties and changing into costumes. The ornately painted façade of the tiring-house could serve as the backdrop for a royal court, as in the opening scene of *A Midsummer Night's Dream*. At ground level, the tiring-house offered three modes

Fig 1. *In the large London playhouses, the balcony above the stage could be used for staging, seating, or to house musicians.*

Fig 2. *English Renaissance drama made minimal use of sets or backdrops. In the absence of a set, the stage pillars could be incorporated into the action, standing in for trees and other architectural elements.*

Fig 3. The discovery space, located in the middle of the backstage wall, could be used as a third entrance as well as a location for scenes requiring special staging, such as in a tomb or bedchamber.

Fig 4. A trapdoor led to the area below the stage, known as "Hell" (as contrasted with the painted ceiling, known as "Heaven" or the "heavens"). Ghosts or other supernatural figures could descend through the trap, and it could also serve as a grave.

of access to the stage: two side doors and a larger, central space that could be concealed with a curtain. In *A Midsummer Night's Dream*, when the artisans meet in the forest to rehearse, Quince observes that they can use "[t]his green plot" as a stage and "this hawthorn brake" as a tiring-house (3.1.3–4). Shakespeare cleverly has his audience imagine the actual tiring-house as a hawthorn thicket in the forest that Quince converts into an impromptu tiring-house.

The experience of attending a play at the Theatre or the Globe was markedly different than the typical visit to the theater today. In modern theaters, the illusion that the actors occupy a separate world from the audience is created through a proscenium arch, stage curtains, and the dimming of house lighting at the start of the play. Since Elizabethan open-air theaters had none of these features, playgoers and actors were fully aware of each other's presence. The large capacity of the playhouses, which could accommodate approximately 2,500 people seated in the galleries encircling the stage or standing in the yard at its front and sides, meant that playgoers were a visible, and probably frequently noisy, presence. In *A Midsummer Night's Dream*, the artisans' performance of "Pyramus and Thisbe" provides an exaggerated instance of playgoers' interactions with each other and with the actors. Unlike Duke Theseus's court, however, public theater audiences were socially heterogeneous, and some playgoers might well have found the aristocrats' ridicule of the artisans distressing or offensive.

In a theater without scenery, costume was essential for establishing both geographical place and social place, or rank. Shakespeare's company might have attempted to give Theseus a vaguely classical look or Hippolyta a recognizably Amazon costume, including buskins, or high boots (2.1.71). But as royalty, the Duke and his bride would have certainly worn the rich, ornately decorated clothing of the Elizabethan nobility. The Athenian lovers would have been dressed as fashionable Elizabethan gentlewomen and gentlemen; the artisans whom Robin mocks as "hempen homespuns" would have worn the coarse and simple garb of contemporary tradesmen (3.1.67). Like Snug's lion costume, Bottom's ass head probably featured a large mouth through which his face would be visible and his voice could project. Contemporary descriptions of Robin Goodfellow indicate that he might have been depicted as a satyr or quasi-demonic figure, with a rough calfskin suit and red face paint. The Fairy's reference to Robin as a "lob" or country bumpkin suggests that a larger actor, probably an adult, played the role (2.1.16). Because the fairies are described as small enough to hide in "acorn cups," they might have been played by boys (2.1.31). But given the stretch of imagination required to imagine even a small boy as a miniscule fairy, the four adult actors who played the roles of the minor artisans might have also doubled as fairies.

Since the Elizabethan theater was primarily an aural as opposed to a visual performance space, playgoers were probably sharply attuned to contrasts of verbal style. At the beginning of the play, for instance, Egeus's comically agitated charges against Hermia and Lysander provide a vivid counterpoint to Theseus's measured pronouncements about nuptial pomp. Distinct styles of speech might also provide insight into characters' social rank, disposition, or present mental state. Hermia and Lysander convey their passion by speaking in *stichomythia*, or rapidly alternating lines (1.1.135–140). Hermia's shift to rhyming couplets imparts an appropriate formality to her vow of love (1.1.171–178), yet when Helena enters, all three characters continue to speak in couplets. The highly artificial style of their conversation emphasizes the conventionality of their distress as stereotypically thwarted lovers.

The lyrical speech of the lovers contrasts sharply with the prose spoken by the commoners in the following scene. When

Bottom does speak verse, it is only to imitate the hyperbolic rant of the stage tyrant. Nonetheless, Bottom's language is not the plain prose of everyday speech, for it is enhanced with hilarious malapropisms and bawdy puns. The actors who played the artisans doubtless indulged in some improvised clowning. The famous clown Will Kemp played Bottom, and we can well imagine him initiating a roaring match with Snug in order to prove his ability to play the lion's part. Flute's presumably exaggerated miming of feminine speech and gestures for Thisbe would have contrasted with the more naturalistic impersonation of femininity by the trained boy actors who took the play's female roles. Since the use of boy actors for female roles was conventional, most playgoers probably did not remain consciously aware that a Helena or Hermia was really male. However, an overtly erotic episode, such as Titania's dotage on Bottom, might have sparked a playgoer's awareness of observing a cross-dressed boy courting an adult man.

The distinctive language and appearance of the fairies usher the audience into the evocative world of a nighttime forest. In Act One, the lovers and artisans announce their plans to meet "tomorrow night" in the woods "by moonlight" (1.1.164, 1.2.88–89). Illuminated by the afternoon sun, an Elizabethan theater could represent neither darkness nor moonlight, and it is unlikely that actors or stagehands interrupted the rapid flow of the action by carrying prop trees onto the stage. (That the artisans try to compensate for the theater's limited technical resources by casting actors as Moonshine and Wall proves their naiveté.) Instead, Shakespeare indicates the shift of locale from city to forest by having a spirit recount, in songlike poetry, his wanderings through hills and bushes. Robin's reference to hostile encounters between Titania and Oberon "in grove or green, / By fountain clear or spangled starlight sheen" not only provides plot information, but also gorgeously evokes the natural setting (2.1.28–29). The initial appearance of Oberon and Titania emphasizes the grandeur of this imaginary setting, as they make simultaneous, symmetrical entrances from the doors on either side of the tiring-house façade. Courtiers in tow, the King and Queen of fairies sweep dramatically across the great empty platform to confront each other at center stage.

Featuring complex interactions of various character groupings, the forest scenes require easily legible orchestrations of bodies and sounds. In Act Four, scene one, for instance, the four lovers remain asleep on stage, possibly against the tiring-house wall, while Titania caresses Bottom at the front of the stage. Observing Titania from behind, Oberon finally releases her from the love spell and asks her to dance. The music for the play's many dances and songs was probably performed in the upper gallery of the tiring-house. Music was also used to create atmospheric contrasts. For instance, the rustic "tongs and bones" Titania provides for Bottom's entertainment would have sounded much harsher than the fairy music (possibly soft recorders) that she calls for here to charm the mortals to sleep. After their dance, the fairies exit, at which point the sounding of hunting horns signals the arrival of day and of Theseus's party, who discover and rouse the four sleeping lovers. Finally, Bottom is left alone on stage to awaken and recount his dream.

Shakespeare's comedies typically end with a communal celebration such as a dance or banquet. In *A Midsummer Night's Dream*, not only do the fairies sing and dance to bless Theseus's house, but Bottom and (probably) Flute conclude the performance of "Pyramus and Thisbe" with a bergomask, a vigorous country dance that would have given Will Kemp an opportunity to display his noted athletic skills. Like many performances on the public stage, *A Midsummer Night's Dream* probably concluded with yet another entertainment called a jig, a bawdy song-and-dance routine unconnected to the subject matter of the play. Imagine what it might have been like to see the actor who had just played the authoritative and restrained Duke Theseus return to the stage to dance an irreverent jig.

Significant Performances
by Mario DiGangi

1595–1596 Because *A Midsummer Night's Dream* concludes with the performance of a play at an aristocratic wedding, some believe that it was originally performed at the wedding celebration of a noble couple, perhaps in the presence of Queen Elizabeth. However, there is no evidence that the play was performed on such an occasion, and no such occasion is necessary to explain the play's origin or subject matter. When *A Midsummer Night's Dream* was first published in 1600, its title page indicated that the play had been "sundry times publicly acted," presumably in The Theatre. The courtier Dudley Carleton reported that he saw "a play of Robin goode-fellow" at court in January 1604: this play might have been *A Midsummer Night's Dream*, but we have no way of knowing for sure.

1661 The comic scenes of *A Midsummer Night's Dream* were extracted to form the core of *The Merry Conceited Humours of Bottom the Weaver*, a droll (brief comic sketch) that was performed during the interregnum, when the public theaters in England were officially closed, and printed in 1661. Focused on clowning, this droll excised altogether the romantic plot concerning the young lovers. It was one of many radical adaptations of the play—centered primarily either on the artisans or the fairies—that dominated the English stage until the mid-nineteenth century.

1662   This is the only known Restoration production of *A Midsummer Night's Dream*. The diarist Samuel Pepys described it as "the most insipid ridiculous play that ever I saw in my life." However, he conceded that he enjoyed "some good dancing and some handsome women." After 1660 women, not boys, played the female roles on the English stage.

1692   The Restoration taste for lavishly produced opera is evident in *The Fairy Queen*, adapted by Thomas Betterton with the music of Henry Purcell. This semi-opera severely cut and reorganized Shakespeare's text and added characters (fawns and naiades, a chorus of Chinese men and women, Night, woodmen) in order to provide greater opportunities for dances, songs, pageants, and the spectacular scenic effects made possible by technical advances in theater design. Until the early twentieth century, productions of *A Midsummer Night's Dream* regularly exploited the spectacle of the play's exotic settings—classical Athens and/or the fairy-haunted forest—through music, dances, and sumptuous scenery.

1716   Richard Leveridge wrote the music for a *Comic Masque of Pyramus and Thisbe*, a parody of the current English taste for Italian opera.

1755   Produced by David Garrick at the Theatre Royal in Drury Lane, with music by George Handel's student John Christopher Smith, *The Fairies* was an operatic treatment of the play that eliminated the mechanicals completely (hence eliminating Act Five), instead focusing on the four lovers and the fairies, who were played by children.

1763   Garrick's company mounted a disastrous revival of *A Midsummer Night's Dream* that cut out the entire last act of the play and rewrote the lovers' dialogue to eliminate rhyme; the play saw only one performance.

1816 Frederic Reynolds emphasized comedy and spectacle in his heavily rewritten and reorganized adaptation of the play for the Theatre Royal in Covent Garden. Moving "Pyramus and Thisbe" to Act Three, he concluded the play with a "Grand Pageant" commemorating Theseus's heroic triumphs over the Centaurs and the Minotaur. Reynolds's adaptation was revised in 1833 with a musical overture by Felix Mendelssohn. Mendelssohn's complete score for the play (first performed in a Berlin production of 1843) had an enormous impact on productions of *A Midsummer Night's Dream* during the next hundred years.

1840 Actor-manager Madame Vestris played Oberon in this Covent Garden production that greatly influenced Victorian stagings of the play. Vestris restored most of Shakespeare's text, although she cut hundreds of lines from the lovers' dialogue, which she regarded as too racy. She established a trend for setting the play in a recognizably classical Athenian locale through the use of properties, scenic painting, and costumes. Typical of Victorian treatments of the play, Vestris's production used elaborate scenic effects (such as a setting moon and sunrise at the end of Act Four) to portray a gorgeously realistic forest, which was populated with ballet-dancing fairies and a female Robin Goodfellow.

1856 Charles Kean placed even greater emphasis on the visual aspects of the play than had Madame Vestris. He cut almost half of Shakespeare's text, particularly from the lovers' speeches, on the grounds of decorum. In place of dialogue, Kean added magnificent dances and pageantry: sixty (adult) fairies accompanied Oberon and Titania onstage, and the conclusion of Act Three was marked by a fairy ballet around a maypole. Concerned to provide a historically authentic depiction of classical Athens, Kean used painted backdrops of Greek landmarks such as the Theater of Bacchus and the Acropolis.

1900   The apotheosis of the Victorian staging tradition, Herbert Beerbohm Tree's production transformed *A Midsummer Night's Dream* into a lavish sensual feast. Athens was represented by painted scenery of massive marble temples, while the forest featured singing mechanical birds, a simulated creek, moonlight peering through a lush canopy of trees, and, in the 1911 revival, live rabbits.

1909   The Brooklyn-based Vitagraph Company produced the first of several silent film versions of *A Midsummer Night's Dream*. Running only eleven minutes, the film, shot outdoors, attempts to capture the comic spirit of the play in scenes focusing on the fairies and the artisans.

1914   Sweeping away the excesses of Victorian realism, Harley Granville Barker's groundbreaking and controversial production made a powerful impact through an emphasis on Shakespeare's text and on non-representational imagery. Instead of Mendelssohn's music, Barker used English folk tunes. The fairies were no longer ballet dancers. Attired in golden Asiatic costumes and gold face-paint, they seemed as "solid as gilt statues," as one reviewer marveled, and they conveyed invisibility by standing motionless on stage. Barker's scenery and staging utilized emblematic, symmetrical forms: white silk curtains embellished with a grapevine pattern represented Athens; green and purple silk curtains represented the forest.

1935   Directed by Max Reinhardt, this Warner Brothers film followed the Victorian tradition with Mendelssohn's music, gauzy white-attired fairies, and spectacular ballet sequences. The well-known

Hollywood cast featured James Cagney (Bottom), Mickey Rooney (Puck, i.e., Robin), and Olivia de Haviland (Hermia).

1959 Intent on producing new interpretations of Shakespeare for the modern age, Peter Hall presented a rougher, edgier *A Midsummer Night's Dream* at Stratford. As in Barker's 1914 production, balletic fairies were banished: Hall's fairies were gritty and impish. Clumsy, confused, and awkward, the young lovers behaved in a more naturalistic manner than the elegantly versifying young gentles of tradition. Fusing a modern interpretation of the play with elements borrowed from its original staging, Hall set the play in an Elizabethan manor house, and used Elizabethan costumes, instrumental music, and folk tunes.

1960 Benjamin Britten's three-act opera closely follows Shakespeare's text, although it opens not with the Athenian court but with the conflict between Oberon and Titania; Theseus and Hippolyta appear only in the final act. Britten evokes the eeriness of the forest world by casting Oberon as a countertenor and Puck (i.e., Robin) as a non-singing role; setting the fairy voices in high registers; and scoring the fairies' music to distinctive instruments (harpsichord, harps, celesta, and light percussion).

1969 Based on his 1959 stage production (and its 1962 revival), Peter Hall's film rejected the whimsy of the Victorian tradition. Hall's handheld camera work, muddy forest setting, and rather demonic-looking Puck (i.e., Robin) all stress the less refined aspects of sexual desire. The film featured Royal Shakespeare Company actors such as Diana Rigg (Helena), Helen Mirren (Hermia), Judi Dench (Titania), and Ian Holm (Puck).

1970 In the most celebrated twentieth-century production of *A Midsummer Night's Dream* (and arguably of any Shakespeare play), Peter Brook revolutionized the modern theatrical approach to Shakespeare. Radically departing from both historical and naturalistic approaches, Brook demonstrated the power of staging Shakespeare conceptually, by using striking stage images that would convey the essence of an idea. For Brook, *A Midsummer Night's Dream* was about eroticism, vitality, and virtuosic theatrical magic. The set was a simple white box consisting of three walls; during the performance, the fairies as well as musicians and stagehands appeared on a catwalk above the set. For the forest scenes, spiraled metal wires representing trees, trapezes for the fairies, and a huge red feather for Titania's bower were lowered over the stage. The fairies were clad in simple, vibrant costumes inspired by the Chinese circus: Puck (i.e., Robin) in yellow, Oberon in purple, Titania in green. The acting was highly athletic and overtly sexual, as indicated in an often-reproduced photograph from the production in which a fairy thrusts his forearm between Bottom's legs to simulate an erection. When Puck spoke his final lines—"Give me your hands," a conventional bid for applause—the actors left the stage to shake hands with the audience in a spirit of comic communion.

1986 Influenced by the Freudian theory of the unconscious, some twentieth-century productions of *A Midsummer Night's Dream* have emphasized the psychology of dreaming. For his Royal Shakespeare Company production, Bill Alexander conceived of the play's forest episode as Hippolyta's dream, a manifestation of a respectable woman's longing for excitement and sexual fulfillment. A long, shared look between Hippolyta and Bottom as he arrived for rehearsal signaled the transition from the elegant 1930s Art Deco setting of the Athenian scenes to the fantastic dream world of the forest. When Hippolyta entered the forest, across which a giant spiderweb was slung, fairies removed her gown, transforming her into a black-clad Titania.

1992 Robert LaPage's strongly conceptual experimental production at the Royal National Theatre stressed the darkness, danger, and eroticism of dreams. The play opened with Theseus and Hippolyta perched on the edge of an iron bed in which the four lovers were sleeping. Illuminated by a bare hanging lightbulb, a large, muddy pool of water occupied center stage. Having engaged in overtly sexual, muddy romping during the forest scenes (a feature that caused critics to dub the production "a mudsummer nightmare" and "the wet dream"), the lovers signaled their departure from their dream state by taking a collective shower at the back of the stage at the end of Act Four.

1994 Paying homage to the energetically physical spirit of Brook's production, Adrian Noble's Royal Shakespeare Company production used a red box set; brightly colored, eastern-inspired, costumes; and trapezes made of huge inverted umbrellas for the fairies, including a pink-pillowed bower for Titania. Hanging lightbulbs adorned the forest. The surreal merger of the mortal and fairy worlds was suggested by elements of scenery and staging, as well as by the doubling of parts between Theseus and Oberon, Hippolyta and Titania, and the artisans and fairies. The production stressed the overt sexual attraction not only between Titania and Bottom but also between Oberon and Puck (i.e., Robin). Noble's 1996 made-for-television film of the production framed the action of the play as the dream of a young boy.

1999 Michael Hoffman set his film of *A Midsummer Night's Dream* in a late nineteenth-century Tuscan village. As a clumsy, bicycle-riding Helena, Calista Flockhart contrasts sharply with Michelle Pfeiffer's radiant and serene Titania. Kevin Kline plays Bottom sympathetically as a foppishly white-suited would-be actor humiliated by teenagers and harassed by a demanding wife.

2001   Director Christine Edzard attempted to capture a sense of the play's innocence and wonder by casting her film of *The Children's Midsummer Night's Dream* with London grade-school children.

2003   Featuring an all-male cast, Edward Hall's Watermill Theater-Propeller production made no attempt to disguise the gender of the actors playing female roles: the men did not wear wigs or imitate women's voices. The vigorous performances stressed the raucous humor of the play's physical comedy, and the innovative set—white ladders draped with white sheets and topped with rows of white chairs—set off colorful costumes such as the red-and-white striped tights Puck (i.e., Robin) wore under his tutu.

Further Reading

Griffiths, Trevor R., ed.   *Shakespeare in Production: A Midsummer Night's Dream.* Cambridge: Cambridge University Press, 1996.

Rothwell, Kenneth S. *A History of Shakespeare on Screen: A Century of Film and Television.* 2nd ed. Cambridge: Cambridge University Press, 2004.

Styan, J. L. *The Shakespeare Revolution: Criticism and Performance in the Twentieth Century.* Cambridge: Cambridge University Press, 1977.

Williams, Gary Jay. *Our Moonlight Revels: A Midsummer Night's Dream in the Theatre.* Iowa City: University of Iowa Press, 1997.

Inspired by *A Midsummer Night's Dream*

W hen *A Midsummer Night's Dream* was first performed for Elizabethan audiences probably in 1596—shortly after Shakespeare's great tragedy *Romeo and Juliet*—the "pleasant comedy" could easily have been dismissed as slight and shallow. While it alluded to great literary works such as Ovid's *Metamorphoses* and Chaucer's *A Knight's Tale*, Shakespeare's play full of fairies and spells might have been thought too foolish to garner the attention of the serious theatergoer. The play was remarkable, however, for featuring a plot entirely of Shakespeare's own creation, rather than being an adaptation of an existing story. Over time, even the well-established fairy characters of Oberon, Titania, and the roguish Robin Goodfellow (also known as Puck, though technically this designates a type of mischievous spirit rather than serves as a proper name) became indelibly associated with Shakespeare's giddy tale of fairy mischief and carnal riot. While the reputation of the play has fluctuated over the centuries, it is currently one of Shakespeare's most beloved and often performed plays. The musical, crystalline language of *A Midsummer Night's Dream* and the heady, imaginative world it evokes have inspired generations of artists in every medium.

Theater

Not long after Shakespeare's death in 1616, abridged versions of *A Midsummer Night's Dream* began to appear on London stages. *The Merry Conceited Humours of Bottom the Weaver,* presented in London in 1661, presented a drastically cut rendition of Shakespeare's text consisting only of the rude mechanicals' play rehearsals. The larger, framing story of the human and fairy lovers was completely eliminated, resulting in a backstage farce that focused on the tradesmen's mishaps as they attempt to stage "Pyramus and Thisbe."

Another liberal cutting of the play appeared in 1692, when British composer Henry Purcell presented his semi-opera *The Fairy Queen.* This interpretation did away with the players altogether, focusing instead on the lovers and the fairies. Purcell, who composed the music for the piece in the Baroque style for which he was well known, removed large sections of Shakespeare's text and replaced scenes with songs and dances. Highlighting the sensational visual aspects of Shakespeare's story, Purcell's masque concluded with a grand spectacle in Act Five, which involved the Roman goddess Juno, a chorus of Chinese singers, and a dance performed by monkeys.

While most interpretations of *Midsummer* are lighthearted, some choose to emphasize the darker, occult elements of the play's magic. Such is the case with *Faust,* by the German poet and playwright Johann Wolfgang Goethe. In one part of the play, Faust and Mephistopheles (the devil to whom Faust has sold his soul) travel to a mountain peak for a witches' celebration where they are entertained by a play entitled *The Golden Wedding Anniversary of Oberon and Titania.* While Goethe would have been familiar with the characters of Oberon and Titania from other literary sources, the presentation of their marriage as a play-within-a-play alludes to Shakespeare, who was widely read in German during Goethe's lifetime. In this context, the playgoers are associated with Satan, and the ritual is not a royal wedding but a pagan rite. This macabre twist on the central characters of *Midsummer* speaks to the occasionally precarious position magic held in the Christian world of Shakespeare and Goethe.

Perhaps the most successful modern adaptation of Shakespeare's play, *The Donkey Show* ran Off-Broadway from 1999 to 2005 at the El Flamingo dance club in New York City. Aptly subtitled *A Midsummer Night's Disco*, this quasi-musical has Shakespeare's characters lip-syncing to popular disco tunes such as "Car Wash," "Don't Leave Me This Way," and "You Sexy Thing." Set in a disco owned by Oberon, *The Donkey Show* abandons Shakespeare's text in its depiction of the polymorphous sexuality and rampant drug use of the 1970's club culture. Helen, Dimitri, Mia, and Sander are clubgoers who play out their love quadrangle on the dance floor, singing and dancing among the audience members. To make way for the actors, the audience is maneuvered around the club by Titania's fairies, portrayed here as scantily clad, well-muscled men. Created by Diane Paulus and Randy Weiner, this adaptation transforms Puck (i.e., Robin) into a rollerskating drug pusher and splits Bottom into two polyester-suited men (both named Vinnie).

Music and Dance

Though Shakespeare's *Midsummer* was rarely performed in Europe during the eighteenth and early nineteenth centuries, German composer Felix Mendelssohn premiered his now famous *Overture to A Midsummer Night's Dream* in April 1827. The text of Shakespeare's play was commonly taught in schools, however, and Mendelssohn and his siblings had studied and performed scenes from the play as children. Mendelssohn would credit Goethe and his reference to *Midsummer* in *Faust* as a major influence on his overture. He assigned specific instruments to illustrate the emotional quality of each character or group of characters: staccato string plucks evoke the flying fairies, brass instruments mirror the unrefined nature of the tradesmen, and the sweeping movements of the combined orchestra conjure the soaring emotion of the young lovers. The *Overture* was so popular that Shakespeare's play gained renewed favor, and in 1843 the King of Prussia commissioned Mendelssohn to compose incidental music for theatrical productions of the play. These compositions were wildly popular and catapulted *Midsummer* from relative obscurity to international fame, resulting in the play being performed throughout Europe, both with and without Mendelssohn's music, for the rest of the century. The *Overture* and *Incidental Music* are among the most famous and recognizable pieces of music in the Western world, particularly the Wedding March, still used as traditional exit music at weddings today.

The first recorded ballet based on *Midsummer* was presented in 1855 at La Scala in Milan, with choreography by Giovani Corsati and music by Paolo Giorza. Subsequent ballets of original choreography, focusing primarily on the young lovers (represented by duets) and the fairies (represented by a troupe of ballerinas, commonly *en pointe*), could be seen throughout Europe from then on. Productions using Mendelssohn's *Overture* and *Incidental* music were presented in St. Petersburg in 1876 and 1906, Paris in 1933, and Brussels in 1955.

In 1962, George Balanchine used Mendelssohn's music to create a full-length, original ballet for an American audience. Like Mendelssohn, Balanchine had grown up with the play, having played a fairy in a theatrical performance in St. Petersburg, Russia, when he was eight years old. Balanchine removed the play-within-a-play subplot and divided the piece into two acts, homing in on the lovers, the magical fairies, and the recurring themes of transformation and fantasy. The production was the New York City Ballet's first performance at the New York State Theater at Lincoln Center, and has since gone on to become the most famous modern dance adaptation of Shakespeare's play.

An opera version of *Midsummer* by the famed British composer Benjamin Britten premiered in 1960 at the Aldeburgh Festival in England. Known for his interest in social and cultural outsiders, Britten uses his complex compositions to emphasize the various distinctions between groups of characters. The players, for example, are given simple, rustic tunes while the wealthier, worldly lovers are underscored by more regal compositions. The fairies in turn are given sweeping, ethereal music, distinguishing them explicitly from the human world. Shakespeare's plotline remains mostly intact in Britten's opera, with the emphasis on collective identity lending the story a new social resonance.

The British rock band Queen cites *Midsummer* in their 1973 hit "My Fairy King," cementing the play's reputation as an ode to rebellious, freethinking youth. The song's lyrics depict a magical ruler who lives in the forest, an omnipotent king with the power to transform anything he pleases. A clear allusion to Shakespeare's Oberon, the song goes on to praise the magic of the fairies and lament the trials and tribulations of love.

Film

Ingmar Bergman's 1955 film *Smiles of a Midsummer Night*, set at the turn of the twentieth century, follows a group of couples, ex-couples, and potential future couples on a weekend trip to the Swedish countryside. Bergman focuses on the story's human lovers, eschewing both the players and the fairies. The rural excursion parallels the Athenian lovers' trip into the forest, and miscommunications and erotic complications abound in Bergman's film as they do in Shakespeare's play. All the characters are in love with someone other than the person they are partnered with, and pursue the objects of their affection at the expense of their spouses or betrothed—who also happen to be sneaking around on romantic assignations of their own. Stephen

Sondheim adapted the Bergman film for his stage musical *A Little Night Music*, which opened on Broadway in 1973. The musical, which adheres closely to *Smiles of a Midsummer Night*, was released as a film in 1977, directed by Harold Prince.

In 1982, Woody Allen wrote and directed an adaptation of Bergman's film called *A Midsummer Night's Sex Comedy*. Allen's film also uses the setting of a weekend retreat to explore the themes of love, lust, confusion, and infidelity. As in Shakespeare's play, Bergman's film, and Sondheim's musical, couples leave their urban surroundings—in this case, sophisticated, modern New York—for the countryside, where they take turns exchanging romantic partners. In a nod to previous adaptations of the play, Allen uses Mendelssohn's music on the soundtrack.

Celestino Coronado's 1984 film version *A Midsummer Night's Dream* (based on Lindsay Kemp's avant-garde dance piece) experiments freely with the rich visual world evoked by Shakespeare's play. This loose adaptation only keeps about a third of Shakespeare's text and incorporates music, modern dance, and visual art to create an anachronistic world with no definitive time, place, or social hierarchy. Lindsay Kemp (who was David Bowie's mime teacher for the rock star's iconic *Ziggy Stardust* concerts) is a major figure in the world of British dance, his work characterized by an erotic, highly physical rock-and-roll exuberance. In Kemp's *Midsummer*, Titania is played by a drag queen while Helena, Hermia, Lysander, and Demetrius pair off briefly into same-sex couples before returning to the outside world and conventional sexual relationships.

Midsummer makes a pointed appearance in Peter Weir's 1989 film *Dead Poets Society*, about a group of young men attending a strict American boarding school in the 1950s. Inspired by their progressive, eccentric English teacher, the boys defy authority by sneaking off into the nearby forest and reading poetry to one another. When the school puts on a production of *Midsummer*, one of the students plays the role of Puck (i.e., Robin) despite his strict father's disapproval. When the boy's father, unmoved by his son's inspired performance, tells him that he's going to be pulled out of the boarding school and enrolled in a military academy, the young man commits suicide. Like many modern interpretations of *A Midsummer Night's Dream*, *Dead Poets Society* emphasizes the play's romantic, impulsive nature, as both works celebrate the youthful desire for freedom.

Visual Arts

In their depictions of *Midsummer*, visual artists have tended to focus primarily on the fairy world. Painter, author, philosopher, and mystic William Blake painted numerous scenes from the play, most notably *Oberon, Titania, and Puck* (1785). This watercolor of a joyous fairy dance is significant not only for the serene, ethereal quality of its sweeping lines and pastel colors but also because no major productions of *Midsummer* had been staged in Europe since 1686, and wouldn't again be until 1826.

Around the same time as Blake, the British artist Henry Fuseli painted a series of *Midsummer* portraits focusing on Titania's deluded affair with Bottom. In *Titania and Bottom* (1786–1789), a fair, nearly naked Queen calls upon her attendants to minister to her new beloved, who sits pensively looking at a tiny fairy in the palm of his hand. In *Titania, Bottom and the Fairies* (1793–1794), Titania clings lovingly to the large, masculine-looking Bottom, who sits demurely with his ankles pulled up to his chest. An earlier painting, *Titania's Awakening* (1785–1789) depicts the moment when Titania wakes to tell her husband, Oberon, of the strange dream she has had. Oberon and Titania stand on the left side of the canvas, bathed in an ethereal light, while Bottom lies sleeping in the right-hand corner, shadowed and surrounded by sinister-looking elves and demons.

The Victorian painter Richard Dadd, like many artists during that period, was preoccupied with fairy lore and often took characters from *Midsummer* as his subjects. His complex, dark compositions generally depict a cluttered, fractured world, but in *Titania Sleeping* (1841) he portrays the fairy Queen as a glowing symbol of womanly perfection, surrounded by caretakers and protected by a series of sprites. In *Puck and the Fairies* (1841), a childlike Puck (i.e., Robin) sits on a toadstool surrounded by dancing fairies. Dadd spent the latter half of his adult life hospitalized in a mental institution, where he painted *Contradiction: Oberon and Titania* (1854–1858), an obsessively detailed depiction of Act Two, scene one where the fairy monarchs clash over the disputed Indian changeling, as well as his masterpiece *The Fairy-Feller's Master Stroke* (1855–1864), which features a small detail of Titania and Oberon overlooking a fatherly, white-bearded figure Dadd referred to as "The Patriarch."

In 1991, Neil Gaiman's critically acclaimed *Sandman* comic book series (1988–1996) produced an issue based on *A Midsummer Night's Dream*, which went on to become the only comic book ever to win the prestigious World Fantasy Award. Morpheus, the King of Dreams (the Sandman of the series's title), has contracted Shakespeare to write two plays "celebrating dreams," in return for which he will grant the playwright unmatched literary prowess. In this issue, Shakespeare and his company have been brought to "the downs of Sussex" to perform the first of those plays, *A Midsummer Night's Dream*, for an audience of fairies that includes the real Titania, Auberon (as Gaiman spells his name), and Robin Goodfellow. Shakespeare's young son Hamnet has been brought along as well, and while his distant father ignores him, the child catches the attention of the beautiful fairy Queen, Titania, thereby linking Hamnet to the Indian changeling boy of *Midsummer*. The final panel of the comic notes that Hamnet died a few years after *Midsummer* was written, suggesting that the sacrifice of his son was an unexpected consequence of Shakespeare's supernatural contract. The final issue of the *Sandman* series concerns the second of Shakespeare's contracted plays: *The Tempest*.

Puck magazine, the first humor periodical in the United States, took its name from Oberon's mischievous henchman, who had been famous in English folklore as Robin Goodfellow long before his star turn in Shakespeare's play. The name "Puck" had become synonymous with mischief, pranks, and trouble. The magazine, famous for its political cartoons, caused mischief from the streets of New York City to the Vatican to the White House from 1876 until its final publication in 1918. It was the forerunner of such publications as *National Lampoon* and *The Onion*.

For Further Reading
by Mario DiGangi

Barber, C. L. "May Games and Metamorphoses on a Midsummer Night." In *Shakespeare's Festive Comedy: A Study of Dramatic Form and Its Relation to Social Custom.* Princeton: Princeton University Press, 1959. In his influential study of how the social customs of Elizabethan holidays shaped Shakespearean drama, Barber argues that both aristocratic wedding pageantry and popular May Games provide the familiar cultural material that informs the play's exploration of the folly—and the fertile creativity—of the imagination.

Barkan, Leonard. "Ovid 'Translated.'" In *The Gods Made Flesh: Metamorphosis and the Pursuit of Paganism.* New Haven: Yale University Press, 1986. Regarding *A Midsummer Night's Dream* as Shakespeare's "fullest attempt to respond to the inspirations afforded by Ovidian materials and to translate them into his own mythic language," Barkan examines how the play subjects characters of all ranks and kinds to the transformations worked by the "perils and delights of love."

Bate, Jonathan. "Comedy and Metamorphosis." In *Shakespeare and Ovid*. Oxford: Oxford University Press, 1993. For Bate, *A Midsummer Night's Dream* represents Shakespeare's "most luminous" transformation of the ancient figures and motifs of Ovidian myth into a modern popular drama that incorporates materials from native folklore and that directly addresses Elizabethan social and political concerns.

Boehrer, Bruce. "Shakespeare's Beastly Buggers." In *Shakespeare Among the Animals: Nature and Society in the Drama of Early Modern England*. New York: Palgrave, 2002. Focusing on the play's central image of a "bestial prodigy"—Titania's desire for a man/ass— Boehrer argues that Oberon's paradoxically moralistic and salacious punishment of his wife points to a familiar anxiety in Shakespeare's culture: the fear that human nature, far from being fundamentally distinct from animal nature, is in fact "in constant danger of corruption from the bestial and/or female other."

Calderwood, James L. "*A Midsummer Night's Dream*: Anamorphism and Theseus' Dream." *Shakespeare Quarterly* 42 (1991): 409–430. Calderwood regards Oberon and Titania as the shadowy "doubles" of Theseus and Hippolyta: through the fairies' conflict in the forest (the subject of "Theseus's dream"), Theseus can express and resolve his anxieties about marrying an Amazon, who might be expected to resist her new roles as wife and mother.

Garber, Marjorie. "Spirits of Another Sort: *A Midsummer Night's Dream*." In *Dream in Shakespeare: From Metaphor to Metamorphosis*. New Haven: Yale University Press, 1974. For Garber, the play's self-consciously theatrical exploration of dreaming conveys its "central theme of the dream which is truer than reality"; through insight into the true "visions" they experience, the characters in the play learn the value of imagination, thereby achieving self-knowledge.

Hendricks, Margo. "'Obscured by Dreams': Race, Empire and Shakespeare's *A Midsummer Night's Dream.*" *Shakespeare Quarterly* 47 (1996): 37–60. Critiquing a production of *A Midsummer Night's Dream* that presented the changeling boy as a "rich oriental 'trifle' accessible to the gaze of predominantly white audiences," Hendricks argues that this staging reproduces the play's linkage of fairyland with the imperialist fantasy of India as a site of sexual, religious, and racial difference.

Holland, Norman N. "Hermia's Dream." In *Representing Shakespeare: New Psychoanalytic Essays*, edited by Murray M. Schwartz and Coppélia Kahn. Baltimore: Johns Hopkins University Press, 1980. Holland takes Hermia's dream of the devouring snake as an opportunity to illustrate three different ways of using psychoanalytic theory in literary interpretation: to reveal the unconscious fears and desires of a fictional character; to explore themes that structure the overall text (here, the ambivalence surrounding the separation and fusion of lovers); or to make explicit the reader's own process of constructing the text according to his or her own psychic investments and associations.

Howard, Skiles. "Hands, Feet, and Bottoms: Decentering the Cosmic Dance in *A Midsummer Night's Dream.*" *Shakespeare Quarterly* 44 (1993): 325–342. Contesting the assumption that dancing in the play monolithically signifies social harmony, Howard argues that the play's representation of a clash between elite dancing traditions (associated with Oberon) and popular dancing traditions (associated with Titania) undermines the stability of class and gender hierarchies.

Lamb, Mary Ellen. "Taken by the Fairies: Fairy Practices and the Production of Popular Culture in *A Midsummer Night's Dream*." *Shakespeare Quarterly* 51 (2000): 277–312. In this analysis of the political uses of popular culture in Renaissance England, Lamb argues that the socially disempowered used fairy lore as "white lies" to justify sexual transgressions and robberies; by making his fairies into more benevolent, courtly figures, Shakespeare dampens the subversive power of fairy stories as "weapons of the weak."

Leinwand, Theodore B. "'I Believe We Must Leave the Killing Out': Deference and Accommodation in *A Midsummer Night's Dream*." In *A Midsummer Night's Dream: Critical Essays*, edited by Dorothea Kehler. New York: Routledge, 1998. Leinwand finds that the play provides a critical perspective on relations of power in Elizabethan society through its sympathetic portrayal of the social ambitions and anxieties of the artisans, who (like Shakespeare's acting company) employ strategies of accommodation and deference when confronting their social superiors.

Levine, Laura. "Rape, Repetition, and the Politics of Closure in *A Midsummer Night's Dream*." In *Feminist Readings of Early Modern Culture: Emerging Subjects*, edited by Valerie Traub, M. Lindsay Kaplan, and Dympna Callaghan. Cambridge: Cambridge University Press, 1996. Levine argues that sexual violence defines the worlds of both Athens and the forest; although Theseus initially turns to theater as a means of concealing or managing his sexual conquest of Hippolyta, the play suggests that theater itself, as practiced by the mechanicals and the fairies, aggravates and deepens sexual violence.

Montrose, Louis. "The Shaping Fantasies of *A Midsummer Night's Dream.*" In *The Purpose of Playing: Shakespeare and the Cultural Politics of the Elizabethan Theatre.* Chicago: University of Chicago Press, 1996. In this elaboration of an earlier, and highly influential, essay on the relationship of Shakespeare's play to the culture from which it emerged, Montrose analyzes the multiple ways in which *A Midsummer Night's Dream* transforms and destabilizes Elizabethan constructions of gender, sexuality, social hierarchy, and political authority.

Neill, Michael. "The World Beyond: Shakespeare and the Tropes of Translation." In *Putting History to the Question: Power, Politics, and Society in English Renaissance Drama.* New York: Columbia University Press, 2000. Emphasizing the meaning of *translation* as a "bearing across"—a crossing of geographical or cultural boundaries— Neill reads Bottom as a traveler to an unfamiliar new world, his simultaneously "poignant and grotesque" rapture a reminder of "how close the marvelous stands to the monstrous."

Parker, Patricia. "'Rude Mechanicals': *A Midsummer Night's Dream* and Shakespearean Joinery." In *Shakespeare from the Margins: Language, Culture, Context.* Chicago: University of Chicago Press, 1996. Through a meticulous dissection and cultural contextualization of words such as "rude," "mechanical," and "preposterous," Parker defines the play's artisans as disorderly "joiners" of words, materials, and bodies; their pervasive disorder provides an ironic perspective on the play's harmonious conclusion, which depends on the (seemingly) orderly joining of social classes and marital couples.

Paster, Gail Kern, and Skiles Howard. "Female Attachments and Family Ties." In *A Midsummer Night's Dream: Texts and Contexts.* Boston:

Bedford-St. Martin's, 1999. Paster and Howard situate in relationship to the play a number of illuminating primary documents. Topics covered include Amazons, the figure of the "gossip," nuns, Queen Elizabeth, the poet Amelia Lanyer, and family structure during the Renaissance.

Patterson, Annabel. "Bottom's Up: Festive Theory." In *Shakespeare and the Popular Voice*. Oxford: Blackwell, 1989. Setting *A Midsummer Night's Dream* within the context of contemporary social, political, and economic conflicts, Patterson holds that the play "staged its own resistance" to the argument "that festival liberty leads to violence" by investing Bottom with a festive spirit and a "utopian vision" capable of leveling social differences.

Slights, William E. "The Changeling in *A Dream*." *Studies in English Literature, 1500–1900* 28 (1988): 259–272. For Slights, the changeling boy is an "absent presence" who exists precariously on the boundary between humankind and fairykind; as such, he becomes a figure for the "principle of indeterminacy" that surrounds the play's discordant examination of issues such as love, marriage, and social hierarchy.

Traub, Valerie. "The (In)Significance of 'Lesbian' Desire in Early Modern England." In *Erotic Politics: Desire on the Renaissance Stage*, edited by Susan Zimmerman. New York: Routledge, 1992. In the plays of Shakespeare (mainly *A Midsummer Night's Dream* and *As You Like It*) and his contemporaries, Traub argues, female same-sex desire is depicted as socially transgressive only when the women involved are perceived to challenge conventional gender behavior or to resist their expected reproductive roles as wives and mothers.